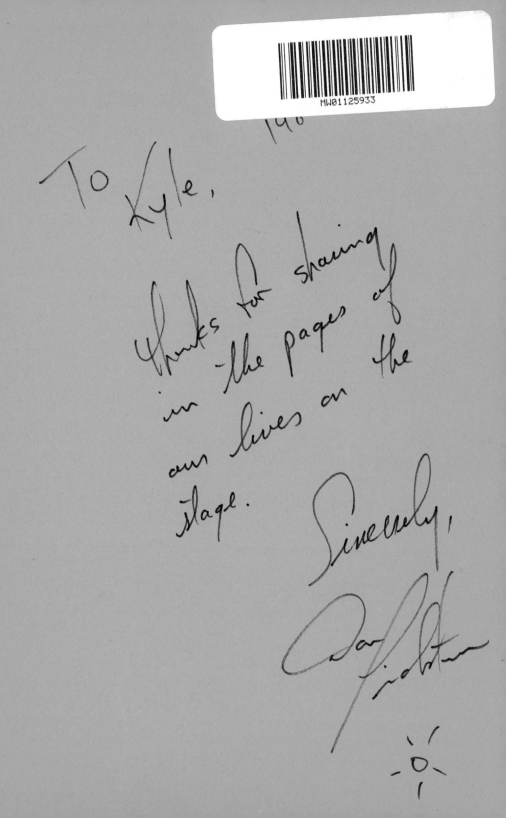

To Kyle,

Thanks for sharing
in the pages of
our lives on the
stage.

Sincerely,

Sun Shade 'n Rain

Moods of Life

Sun Shade 'n Rain

Moods of Life

Dan Lindstrom

Foreword by Paul H. Dunn

Bookcraft

SALT LAKE CITY, UTAH

Library of Congress
Catalog Card Number: 80-67359
ISBN 0-88494-405-0

First Printing 1980

Lithographed in the United States of America
PUBLISHERS PRESS
Salt Lake City, Utah

To the fans of
Sun, Shade 'n Rain —
because of them and for them
this book was written

Foreword

For many years we have heard the admonition from leaders, "Every member a missionary." Sun, Shade 'n Rain have taken that admonition to heart and through music and testimony have shared spiritual truths with thousands. As a result, scores have found the restored Church through the group's singing and speaking talents.

I have long felt that their story should be told. Contained in these pages are delightful accounts of Sun, Shade 'n Rain's many contributions to the lives of people everywhere. I am pleased to recommend this book to all who would care to find religion in a pleasant, enjoyable way.

PAUL H. DUNN

Acknowledgments

I want, first of all, to acknowledge the many Church leaders who have asked Sun, Shade 'n Rain to speak. It was these speaking engagements that led to the writing of this book.

My thanks also go to Mel Teeples, Jeff Gregerson, the entire Sun, Shade 'n Rain organization, and especially our secretary, Sue O'Donnell, who spent many hours proofing and typing my manuscript.

Thanks to Joseph Lake and Clive Romney for their persistent encouragement, constructive criticism, and suggestions.

My list would not be complete without mentioning the great respect I have for Elder Paul H. Dunn and Sun, Shade 'n Rain's musical director, Ron Simpson. Their examples have always been powerful guiding lights for me.

Finally, my gratitude and love go to my family, and especially to my beautiful wife, Charlotte.

Introduction

Many people know who Sun, Shade 'n Rain are, but there are also many people who will pick up this book and ask, "What is Sun, Shade 'n Rain?"

Several years ago three very talented young men Dan Lindstrom, Mel Teeples, and Jeff Gregerson decided they wanted to spend their lives making people happy through music. The Lord had blessed them with great talent, and they wanted to use that talent in giving back to this world a part of themselves.

In trying to decide on a name for this new group, the members wanted one that reflected the type of music they would perform. They wanted to present all kinds and styles of music — music that would please any age group. They did not want to be just another stereotyped rock group, disco group, or middle-of-the-road group. They wanted to share all kinds of music — happy, sad, fast, slow, serious, and funny. They wanted to present it all well and in a way that would genuinely entertain audiences of all ages.

The words *Sun, Shade 'n Rain* best describe the types of music the group performs, and the words also describe the many moods all of us feel throughout our life. Sun for the happy, joyful moods and for the happy, joyful songs. Shade for the mellow moods of life, when things are good and pleasant. Then comes the Rain, the sad, unhappy, tearful times and songs.

Dan, Jeff, and Mel have achieved their goal in all styles of music; and they are true entertainers. In a nightclub in Nevada or New York, at a college show, or at a fair or convention these men captivate the audience yet, at the same time, never lower their own high standards of performance.

These young men are active members of The Church of Jesus Christ of Latter-day Saints (the Mormons). Each of them has served a full-time mission for that Church; Mel and Dan to South Africa, and Jeff to Canada.

Today they are seventies in the Mormon Church (a calling for those in a position to help further the missionary work of the Church), and as of December 1979, they had spoken to over two hundred thousand people in firesides all over this country and in the Islands.

Sun, Shade 'n Rain — Moods of Life has come about because of countless requests for copies of poems, lyrics, and experiences that Dan, Mel, and Jeff have shared with people.

I am proud of these men for the beautiful lives they lead and for the way they unselfishly touch the lives of others. This book is part of that unselfishness.

Joseph G. Lake
Personal Manager of
Sun, Shade 'n Rain

Contents

In the Beginning

Even after thousands of performances, I still get backstage jitters before every concert. I pace around nervously behind the curtains until the music begins. Finally the curtains rise, and the introductions call us onto the stage. As I run out into the lights, all of my butterflies disappear (as if by magic); I relax and do what I love most — perform.

As I approached the beginning of this writing project, I experienced some of those same jitters and fears. I paced around nervously until the day I typed my first word. I had the faith that the curtain would go up as I began writing and that all of my nervousness would go away. It did. The butterflies flew, and I found myself enjoying writing.

This book comes as a result of the many firesides we've done. Many times I have stood at a pulpit and related stories about Sun, Shade 'n Rain and our lives as entertainers. I have often been asked if these experiences were written down. Now they are. I have shared a lot of my personal experiences and the lessons they have taught me.

I read the autobiography of Mahatma Gandhi and was very impressed. In the introductory pages of his history he wrote something that I immediately identified with.

I simply want to tell the story of my numerous experiments with truth . . .

there can be no room for self-praise.
They [the experiments] can only
add to my humility. I hope and pray
that no one will regard the advice
interspersed in the following chapters
as authoritative. The experiments
narrated should be as illustrations, in
the light of which everyone may
carry on his own experiments. (The
Selected Works of Mahatma Gandhi,
ed. Shiriman Narayan, vol. 1
[Ahmedabad-14, India: Navajivan
Press, n.d.], pp. xviii, xix, xxii.)

I accept the blame for any ideas that might be amiss, and yet I share the credit with those who have surrounded me in my life and made all of my experiences what they were.

The entertainment world is a strange one. The pressures are tremendous, and moral standards are nearly nonexistent. In Sun, Shade 'n Rain we survive only by sharing each other's strength. We try to create a "bubble" of protection. We remind each other of our standards and of the things that are truly important in life. If my name ever appeared alone on the marquee, I would have to get out of the entertainment field, because I lean heavily on the help, the support, and the examples of those in Sun, Shade 'n Rain. The experiences in this book revolve around Jeff Gregerson and Mel Teeples, as well as our musicians and the entire staff. I love them all.

I accepted a challenge to write this book, but procrastination and daily commitments kept me from meeting this challenge. The turning point happened in the Sun, Shade 'n Rain office. Our secretary showed me a quote that hit me between the eyes. It simply said, "I knew you couldn't do it," and it was signed by Lucifer. From that moment on I wanted to show Lucifer that I could. I rolled up my sleeves and started writing.

After several months I slipped back into old routines, and my book — only half finished — ended up on the shelf. During this time I met and then married a beautiful girl named Charlotte. She discovered my half-completed book and told me how proud she was of me. It seemed that I could never find time to write the other half until Charlotte said, "Honey, I want to be proud of you for writing the second half, too, but even a mosquito doesn't get a pat on the back until he gets to work." That did it. I went back to work and finished.

One of the main sources of my inspiration was my wife, and I love her dearly. Some of the chapters were written from my "single" point of view, and the better ones from my "married" perspective.

My purpose in writing this book lies in a desire to help others. Life is fascinating, and each person has daily experiences that teach lessons. I hope these pages will help others to look into their own lives and see the magic that's all around.

I know that there is a God. I know that he lives and he loves. He has restored the living, growing Church to the earth. The best pat on the back I could hope for is to know that I might direct a little more glory toward him and to help a few of his children see and recognize him for what he is: a literal Father in Heaven.

As we travel through the moods of life, may we recognize God's hand in all things and acknowledge his influence.

Dan, Jeff,
Mel

The Big Bounce

I get excited every time we fly somewhere, and sometimes this excitement affects others around me. For example, there was the time Sun, Shade 'n Rain was flying out on tour. Our entire staff joined us, and we filled a large section of seats. The stewardess came into the cabin, and as I watched her I was impressed with her demeanor. She was very polite and confident. She had an ability to make people feel relaxed instantly.

For those not familiar with flying procedures, a stewardess serves as a hostess. She welcomes passengers aboard and helps them get seated. Before takeoff she goes through an instructional monologue, describing safety regulations. Then with a smile, she says, "Thank you for flying such and such airlines." Generally, it's the same procedure for all airlines.

As our stewardess carried on with her presentation, we decided that we wanted to do something special for her; something that would make her always remember Sun, Shade 'n Rain. She continued her demonstration, and we quietly discussed our plans. We decided to give her a standing ovation, right there inside the plane, as soon as she finished. We casually unhooked our seat belts; and when she was through showing us how to use our oxygen masks, we jumped to our feet clapping, cheering, and whistling. It was fun to watch our cool, calm, and collected stewardess turn bright red. I'm sure this was an emergency she'd never been trained to handle. She fumbled for something to say and got even more embarrassed when other passengers began to join in the standing ovation. Finally, we all settled down and prepared to take off. I looked at all those other people who had helped us in the applause and wondered about them — what if this was their first flight? They had acted as if it were standard procedure to cheer the stewardess. I laughed to myself as I pictured them on a different flight (without Sun, Shade 'n Rain) trying to repeat the ovation. By the way, we made friends with our flustered stewardess. She and several of her friends came to our concert in Hawaii.

Flying isn't always this enjoyable. I recall one trip when we weren't at all excited to take off. Actually we were nervous. There was no joking around with the stewardess this time. It was December, and we were sitting quietly inside the plane waiting to fly from Salt Lake City to Denver. We had a concert that night, but we were concerned because of the unusually heavy snowstorm. The blizzard was so bad that we had trouble seeing the blinking red lights on the wing tips. I guess we were each secretly hoping that the airline would cancel our flight. They didn't.

Slowly the airplane began to roll, taxiing into position. I took a deep breath, closed my eyes, clutched the armrests, and thought, *I sure hope he knows what he's doing. I have all the faith in the world that our pilot, in fact, knows what he's doing.*

We jerked forward, and the roar of the engines seemed to say "Hold on. Here we go!" Seconds later we were airborne, and as we burst through the clouds I was amazed at what I saw — endless blue sky and a blazing yellow sun. What had happened to the storm? I knew that it was still down there somewhere. I tried to find it, but all I could see was a blanket of fluffy white clouds. It looked like a huge, beautiful carpet of cotton. I could hardly believe that those same white clouds had seemed so frightening only moments earlier.

While we had been trembling in the wind, the cold, and the dark of the storm, our pilot knew that we were only feet away from clear flying. He knew something we didn't, and so he lifted us up. Sure enough, the sun was there and the sky was blue. The ugly clouds had turned beautiful.

Along with a lesson in weather and flying, I learned a great lesson on faith and life. Just as the higher *altitude* made a terrible storm look beautiful, our higher *attitudes* can make the storms of life become beautiful. People who don't think highly of themselves and who habitually stay in the depths of depression and self-pity see only the stormy side of life. If they'd let the Savior be the pilot, they'd find life a much more pleasant trip. The Savior knows something we don't, and each time we let him touch us we are lifted a little higher. Then, just like our plane, we burst through the troubles of life and see things in a new light. Our *attitudes* and our *altitudes* are much the same: as each becomes loftier, the vision becomes clearer.

We, as passengers in life, get to choose. We can stay in the dark and howling storms, or we can rise above them. We can cower under the pressures and storms of life, or we can rise above them. The more our attitudes deal with who we really are and why we're really here, the more our lives are lifted.

When the storms of life come, and they definitely will, it's our positive mental *altitudes* that will allow us to fly through them without crashing. We can rise above the troubles and bask in the ever-present light of the Son. All we need to do is to take a deep breath, close our eyes, clutch the armrests, and say to ourselves, *I have all the faith in the world that he knows what he's doing.* Then the Savior will use that faith and lift us higher and pilot us through the clouds. Our mortal trips are only processes of proving and improving, of rising higher and higher.

The early years of Sun, Shade 'n Rain were struggle years. We often needed part-time work at other jobs to help us get through. Before I went into the entertainment field full time, I worked as a computer operator for one of the large Utah banks. I worked on the graveyard shift and reported at the computer center at midnight. Our computer occasionally broke down, and all the employees on our shift just had to wait until the repairmen arrived and got the machine up again. One of these breakdowns occurred as we were sorting printouts to be shipped to various branches. The twelve of us went on break and waited for the servicemen to do their job. During our free time we usually had full-scale rubber band wars. (To this day, I have a few welts left from those battles.)

This time, however, we didn't flip the rubber bands. Instead, we began with a single, tiny rubber band and rolled it into a tight ball. Then we rolled another rubber band around it, and another around that until we had a solid ball of elastics a little larger than the size of a marble. We made it grow a little larger and larger, one rubber band at a time. All of our free time was spent on the rubber-band-ball project, day after day. Soon it was the size of a golf ball and then a tennis ball. For six months we worked on the project. Finally we were using the largest rubber bands we had available, the eighty-fours.

By now the ball weighed fifty pounds and was about the size of a volleyball. It took two guys to hold it, and a third to stretch the eighty-four around it. The ball was now as big as we could make it, and it was as solid as a rock.

We felt kind of sad when our project was completed. We sat around the lunchroom at three in the morning and looked at each other. There was one question on our minds, "What do we do with a fifty pound rubber-band ball?" The answer was unanimous, "You bounce it!"

Our computer center occupied the three underground floors of the Kennecott Building in downtown Salt Lake City. The cement floor was perfect for "The Big Bounce." Even our supervisor was anxious to see what would happen. We gathered in a large circle for the ceremony. All was ready and the giant ball was thrown downward. After dropping five or six feet, it bounced all right — it bounced right up and shattered a light fixture in the ceiling. We quickly hid the ball and went back to work, with I-wonder-how-that-happened expressions on our faces.

Several days later, when everything had cooled down, we got out the rubber-band ball again. This time we wanted to see how it would bounce if we threw it down three floors

inside the stairwell. (The three underground floors had an open-air stairwell that went clear to the bottom level cement floor.) During our lunch break we gathered again. People were standing on different stairs at different levels looking into the "drop chamber." Everyone had a good seat to see the great three-floor-rubber-band-ball bounce!

It was spectacular! We all loved it; and I will never forget the loud echoing crash that rang through the air as the ball hit the bottom floor and bounced right back to the third floor. It was all I could do to catch it and hold on to it. We talked about it for days and days. I even dreamed about it, and I described the whole event in my journal.

I even learned a lesson from that bouncing experience. The ball and the thrower were the same for both bounces. It was the same cement floor, it was the same amount of throwing effort, and it was the same time of day — yet the second time the ball bounced three times as high. What made the difference? Only one factor had changed — the altitude. Since we were higher the second time, the same ball covered a lot more distance.

The story isn't over yet. We knew how to get on the roof, nearly eighteen stories above the city street. The twelve of us on our shift drew lots to see which six would go to the roof to throw and which six would go to the streets to receive the first bounce. Our plan was to then switch places and bounce the ball again — we all wanted to experience our creation both coming and going.

I was in the first roof group; I can still remember how warm that summer night was, how clear the sky was, and how quiet the streets were. (At three o'clock in the morning there wasn't much going on in downtown Salt Lake City.) We peered over the edge, looking straight down — it would be a fantastic bounce. We looked up and down the nearby streets to make sure no cars were coming. (Our ball would easily have gone right through the roof of an automobile.) The traffic lights were blinking on and off with their yellows and reds. We saw six tiny figures way down on the street, running around, waiting anxiously. I yelled down that I was ready. I remember thinking that once I tossed the ball over the edge it was their job to get out of the way, because I certainly couldn't aim the thing.

I stepped back, braced myself, and then heaved fifty pounds of rubber out into the air. Down it went. What a thrill! It was big enough that it was easy to see. Luckily it missed a street light by inches, and then it bounced hundreds of feet back into the air. After two bounces the retrievers still couldn't catch it. It bounced past the

Brigham Young monument (now that I think about it, it could easily have taken his head off) and finally came to rest when it bounced over the wall around Temple Square. Since the wall completely surrounds a downtown block and the gates are locked up every night, we couldn't have our second bounce. We had to wait until eight o'clock that morning before we could even get the ball back.

Unfortunately, we got into trouble because our secret bounce wasn't so secret after all. Throughout all our excitement no one thought to mention our plans to the building's night watchman. All he saw was a group of graveyard shift employees running around the downtown streets at 3:00 A.M., looking up at the sky — then he saw a rubber UFO leap into the Temple grounds. He just had to report it. I ended up going into Temple Square to retrieve our now famous rubber-band ball. When my shift ended I walked through the open gate, hoping that no one had stolen our ball; there it was, right out on the lawn. I smiled at all the tourists who were watching me and probably thinking, *So these are the Mormons.*

I'll never forget that experience, and as I look back on it I still see that lesson. It was the same ball, the same building, the same thrower — the same everything, except altitude.

We had gone to the roof, the very top. Up there the view was great, and the results of the bounce were spectacular.

How many of us spend our lives in the basement of life where our best efforts can only break a light or hit a ceiling, when the plan of salvation specifies that we can go up to any floor we want? Our attitudes can rise as high as we want. We are children of God; we can become perfect; we can go to the roof; we can become as God himself. What a thought!

Reaching the roof, reaching perfection is not only possible, it's a commandment (see Matthew 5:48). If perfection is that important, how does one reach the roof? Where does one begin? As he usually does, the Lord answers that question for us. He says to start wherever you are and then move upward "one step at a time." Perfection (the roof) is reached line upon line and precept upon precept (see D&C 98:12, 128:21). Progression is eternal, and there really is a "stairway to heaven." We are all on different floors, but we should all be progressing. No one stands still; we either move up toward the roof, or we slip down toward the basement. Joseph Smith said:

When you climb up a ladder, you must begin at the bottom, and ascend step by step, until you arrive at the top; and so it is with the principles of the gospel — you must begin with the first, and go on until you learn all the principles of exaltation. (History of the Church, 6:306-307.)

The time to start climbing that ladder is now, for we truly are living in the "ladder" days. We can lift our thoughts *if we want to*. We can lift our goals *if we want to*. We can lift our moods and keep ourselves happy *if we want to*. We can aim toward godhood and rise daily *if we want to*. And most important, we can improve and perfect ourselves one day at a time, little by little, *if we want to*.

Richard L. Evans said, "We rise no higher than we think, no higher than we play, no higher than our purpose, no higher than our faith." I was surprised to discover how many of my favorite people understood this principle of climbing. President Harold B. Lee stated, "You cannot lift another soul until you are standing on higher ground than he is." ("Stand Ye in Holy Places," *Ensign*, July 1973, p. 123.) Our challenge, then, is to reach upward for that higher ground (for the roof) and then to reach back to pull others up from behind.

David Starr Jordan wrote, "There is always room at the top, but the elevator is not running." We used the elevator to get to the top of the Kennecott Building, but the celestial kingdom isn't that easy to reach. Stairs always work; and Elder Paul H. Dunn tells us how to use them: "Success and greatness are processes of climbing, and climb you must." (*Discovering the Quality of Success* [Salt Lake City: Deseret Book Company, 1973], p. 15.)

The more we practice climbing, the easier it becomes to climb even higher. Our muscles will not only get stronger, but we will find extra help as the angels of the Most High descend and ascend to give us a hand. Jacob saw angels when he beheld the ladder that extended into heaven. That's the ladder we need to find and climb. President Joseph Fielding Smith gave some this clue on how to take that first step toward perfection. He said:

It is my duty, it is yours, to be better today than yesterday . . . Why? Because we are on that road to perfection . . . no man should attempt to excuse himself because he has this failing or that. If we have a failing, if we have a weakness, there is where we should concentrate, with a desire to overcome, until we master and conquer. (Conference Report, October 1941.)

If we are better today than we were yesterday, we are one rung higher and one step closer. Higher and higher we *must* move. The ladder sometimes seems hopelessly long, but it doesn't matter where we are on the ladder as long as we're moving in the right direction.

Let's not give up. Let's choose to rise. Let's improve. Let's fly above the storms. Let's come out of the basements. Let's go to the roof. Let's steadily climb, and if we fall let's bounce back even higher. Let's go to the roof; and as Zig Ziggler, a great motivational speaker says, "I'll see you at the top!"

In concert

Just Passing Through

Somewhere in Canada two Mormon missionaries walked away from a door that had just been slammed in their faces. Elder Jeff Gregerson and his companion had just given their door approach introductions, and the girl told them she wasn't interested by slamming the door. The elders noticed she was wearing a T-shirt with a picture of Snoopy on it. He was up on his dog house fighting his enemy the Red Baron. Snoopy had his paw in the air and was yelling, "Curse you, Red Baron." As Jeff and his companion turned and walked off the porch, Jeff jokingly stopped on the steps, turned back to the house, lifted his fist into the air, and said, "Curse you, Red Baron."

His companion couldn't believe his ears. He couldn't believe what Elder Gregerson had just said. He turned to Jeff with a look of shock and said, "Elder, I know that the priesthood is pretty powerful, but weren't you being kinda hard on her?" Jeff had no idea what his companion was talking about. The companion spoke up again, "What did you say to that girl?" Jeff quickly repeated the innocent phrase, "Curse you, Red Baron." His companion breathed a sigh of relief. He thought Jeff had said, "I curse you to be barren."

This misunderstanding is classic, and I enjoy the story every time I think about it. What the companion needed was a little more faith in Jeff, even though he didn't quite understand what Jeff had said.

Far too often each of us needs to cultivate a little more faith in the Lord, even though we may not always understand what he says. I learned that lesson just about the time I was getting ready to go on a mission for the LDS Church.

I had turned nineteen, and all my missionary papers had been submitted. I looked forward to my mission call and wondered where I'd serve. Instead of receiving a call, I was notified that something had gone wrong — there had been a mistake. I couldn't go on a mission. Because of the Viet Nam war, there was a limit on how many missionaries could be called at one time. It just wasn't my turn. There were eight of us in the ward, all willing and all eligible to be called on missions. But the Church's quota system stipulated that each ward could send only one missionary every six months. Our bishop solved the problem by drawing lots. Nearly two years passed, and I never drew the short straw. I wondered what the Lord had in mind for me. If not a mission, what? Was it the Army? Was it work? Was it marriage? Was it school? Was it simply a lesson in patience? I didn't know.

After some spiritual searchings, I felt I had received my answer. That answer was music. The Lord knew

that I loved music and performing, and I became convinced that he wanted me to use my talents to be a missionary. I didn't need to be formally called to go and serve in the mission field; the Lord wanted me to stay at home and be a missionary by example. That's what I concluded, and so I organized a musical group. We worked and worked. Two years passed, and we came a long way in the entertainment industry. We earned some important contracts and signed for several large out-of-state concerts. Everything was going just right.

Just when the group was most excited and optimistic about the future, it happened! It was a mission call. I couldn't believe this was happening, and I was upset. How come the Lord wanted me to go now, just when everything looked so good? Because I knew that the Lord wanted me to sing, I thought for sure this call was another mistake. Besides, if he wanted me to go on a mission, he would have called me earlier — back when I was ready. "I can't go now, not now! Things are too good — what am I gonna do?"

It was no mistake. I had, in fact, been called to Africa. I fasted. I prayed. I went. It was the most marvelous experience of my life. My testimony exploded into reality and my spirit grew tremendously. I was able to introduce many wonderful people to the gospel, and I felt a peace inside that I'd never felt before. During those two years I learned a lot about faith. I learned, also, that the Lord knew exactly what he was doing. There were definite reasons why he wanted me in Africa at that specific time. Had I gone on my mission when I thought I should have, I would have completely missed meeting Mel Teeples.

I was able to continue singing throughout a lot of my mission. Mel was serving his mission in Africa at the same time, and we performed together much of the time. We worked together, we sang together, and we dreamed together. We talked often about returning to the States after our missions and creating a new singing group. When Mel and I returned to Salt Lake City, we made those dreams come true — Sun, Shade 'n Rain was born.

I am thankful that I didn't go on my mission according to my timetable. The Lord did exactly what he had to do, even though I complained a lot at first. I didn't understand. He knew, however, that my musical future and success depended on my meeting Mel. Our paths crossed at the right time and at the right place.

When we reached Salt Lake City, we began the organizing process. My brother Wade sang with us until he received his mission call, and we finally solicited the help of Jeff Gregerson, who had just returned from serving his mission in Canada. Dan, Jeff, and Mel became Sun, Shade 'n Rain. That was how it all began. Now, we travel and perform extensively — much more than we ever hoped to.

When we're not on the road with Sun, Shade 'n Rain, we stay at our homes in the Salt Lake area, where we all have beautiful families. I love to visit my parents' house, especially to eat. During one such visit the family members were all sitting around the kitchen table enjoying a superb Sunday meal. Suddenly the telephone rang, and everyone looked excited. "That's him! That's him!" mom yelled. As the call had been previously arranged, we all knew it would be my brother Brad calling from London, England. He was serving his mission there, and he had called to talk to the family. His call was a special event, and the whole family had gathered to chat with him. Some of the family ran downstairs to the other extension. Each of us had the chance to visit briefly.

It was great to hear Brad's voice again. Mom and dad talked last; then the time ran out, and the line was disconnected. As I sat back and watched the folks talk to their son for those last few moments, I was deeply touched. They were huddled together listening and talking into the same receiver. They were so full of love and excitement. It impressed me to hear those last seconds of conversation as they yelled into the phone, "We love you, we love you. Thanks for making us so proud. Is there anything you need? Anything at all? We'll send it. Thanks for calling — it's so good to hear from you. Do a good job, and we'll see you when you get home. We love you — " and click, he was gone.

I watched mom and dad for a long time as they smiled and relived the short conversation over and over again. In fact, all day long I thought about that phone call. I tried to imagine our Heavenly Father and Mother being just as excited to hear from us when we make those long distance prayers home. I'm sure thankful that we can call our heavenly parents as often as we want.

It's a simple thing for me to picture this earth life as a mission field. We are serving here, away from our celestial home and friends. I can hear, in my mind, our heavenly parents saying to each of us. "We love you. Thanks for making us so proud. Is there anything you need? Is there anything we can send you? We think about you all the time. Thanks for calling. Do a good job and we'll see you when you get home. We love you."

The more I reflected on Brad's mission and his phone call, the more I compared the mission field to life here on earth. I thought back on my mission in Africa. Those two years certainly had passed by quickly. My earthly mission also is very short. During my entire two years in Africa, I always knew that I was just passing through and that I would soon return home. Life here on this planet is very similar to those two years — we are just passing through, and no one knows for sure when he will get his release and return to his heavenly home.

James understood our temporary state as earthly missionary travelers when he wrote, "For what is your life? It is even a vapour, that appeareth for a little time, and then vanisheth away." (James 4:14.)

What a powerful and pertinent question James asked: "What is your life?" Is it an honorable mission? Is it productive? Are the struggles being handled well? Is your life such that you can look back from future eternities as a returned missionary and say, "Those were the best years of my life"?

I will never forget the pride I felt as I sat on the stand during my farewell sacrament meeting in my home ward. Everyone was there. They again gathered at the Salt Lake airport when I departed for Africa, and I basked in those last few moments of love and glory. There were hugs and tears from family and friends. They were all crowded together waving their good-byes. I was the center of attention right up until I boarded the plane.

I took my seat, looked out the tiny window, and suddenly felt a lump in my throat and tears in my eyes. I saw mom and dad and both sets of grandparents waving frantically at the plane, not knowing which window was mine. I slowly waved back, knowing they couldn't see me. I watched the most important people of my life fade into the distance as the jet roared down the runway. I felt very lonely — all of a sudden there was no more attention, no more glory, no more smiles from loved ones, and no more wishes of good luck. There was only me, and I was off to the other side of the world to a place I'd never been before. I didn't know anyone there, and suddenly two years looked longer than eternity.

I believe that our "farewells" were similar when we left our heavenly homes to come here. I suspect that we were a little apprehensive about leaving the comforts of a celestial abode to come to this planet — to the other side of the universe — to a mission field called Earth. We'd never been here before, and we would arrive as strangers. It must have been a traumatic experience, especially when we realized that we might not return. No wonder we had to start out as babies; we couldn't have handled it any other way. I can picture our heavenly loved ones gathered around at the celestial airport to send us off with tears of joy and hugs of encouragement. Thank God for long distance prayers and the system of scriptural letters and patriarchal telegrams!

Even though leaving my home and family was difficult at first, I was very excited to be going to Africa on my mission. I knew that was what I had to do. I knew that was where my Heavenly Father wanted me, and I was thankful for the chance to serve. I am sure that we were excited, too, in our heavenly homes to receive our calls to come to this second estate. I'm sure that we received blessings and promises concerning the work we would be able to do here on earth. It might have been a sad thing to leave but, just like my mission to South Africa, we were glad to be going.

Once I relaxed on the plane and realized that there was no turning back, I settled down and began to contemplate the next two years. I made some journal entries and mailed some post cards from our Chicago stopover. I made friends with some of the other elders on my same flight. A few were headed for England, and two were going to New York. Four of us were going to

Africa. We four were just like brothers coming to earth. We were headed for the same mission "home" in Johannesburg to meet our new mission "parents." Sure enough, when we landed, there they were.

Our new parents loved us before even meeting us. They took us home and let us rest from the long journey. Immediately, we felt comfortable and secure even though we were foreigners in a strange land. We had to be oriented to new time schedules, a new money system, new language, new friends, new rules, new goals, new work, new customs, new everything. It was a whole new way of life. Our new parents, however, taught us how to adapt and how to be successful. The mission president and his wife watched over us until we could return to Salt Lake City.

Earthly parents have similar responsibilities with their children. They have the job of watching over and raising them and teaching them how to adapt and become successful. In Africa it was certainly a thrill to call home to Salt Lake. Here on earth it is also a thrill to call and visit personally with Heavenly Father.

General Authorities were often sent from Church headquarters, in Salt Lake City, Utah, to South Africa to guide and counsel the Saints.

Similarly, Heavenly Father sends his messengers, his General Authorities, to earth with instructions.

During my African mission I worked hard, and sometimes I got discouraged and depressed. But I had a simple way to overcome those feelings. Whenever I thought of giving up, I just remembered the day I flew out of the Salt Lake airport. I pictured my loved ones and friends waving good-bye, and I knew I couldn't give up. Everyone at home was praying for me, paying for me, trusting in me, and sacrificing for me. There was no way I could go home dishonorably. How could I let them down? How could I let the Lord down? How could I disappoint my mission parents? How could I let myself down? Whenever I imagined myself going home before my mission work was done, I felt tormented inside. I didn't want to be a failure, and so I immediately got back on my knees and then back to work. I wanted to finish the work I was sent to do.

This mortal, earthly mission is much the same. We should fear returning to the celestial airport in shame with a dishonorable release. We should want to see everyone there to greet us and welcome us back. I want my Heavenly Father to pull me aside, put his arm around my shoulder, and say, "Welcome home, son. You handled yourself well. You handled the little things superbly, and now I've got some great things for you. I'm proud of you. Well done!"

Personally, I have no fear of death. I have a deep knowledge that God lives and that we will, indeed, stand before him to give our homecoming reports. Now is the time to create the "good things" to report on. Since we are just passing through, we need to utilize every moment fully. Our success is dependent on our communication with God, our Father, back home. We can keep in touch with him by reading and rereading his letters and by calling him long distance several times a day.

No matter when our releases come and our mortal missions end, we should be prepared to join the prophets of old in saying: "I have warred a good warfare, walking uprightly before God, for I am now ready. The time of my departure is at hand. I have fought a good fight, I have finished my course, I have kept the faith." (See Alma 1:1; 2 Timothy 4:7.)

What a great way to return home — having warred a good warfare and having fought a good fight! Then, with an embrace of love, our eternal God will say, "Welcome home, welcome home."

At Disneyland

More Precious Than Fine Gold

The Sun, Shade 'n Rain organization is a member of the blood assurance program in Utah. As members we donate a minimal amount of blood each year, and then we, along with our families, are eligible for all the blood we might suddenly need.

Jeff once told the story about a nurse who called him and asked him to donate some blood. Jeff is a regular donor, and the nurse explained that a certain Mr. Green was going to have open-heart surgery and he needed blood. Jeff agreed to give blood and went to the hospital. As he tried to relax on the table, watching his own blood leave his body, Jeff felt glad that he could help. It made him feel good, knowing that his blood would help save the life of Mr. Green. Then a strange idea came into Jeff's mind, and he laughed to himself as he wondered what would have happened if he hadn't showed up. What if Jeff had decided not to keep the appointment and had gone to a movie instead of the hospital.

He continued to chuckle as he pictured the nurse tiptoeing into the operating room and tapping the doctor on the shoulder. "Yes, nurse, what is it?"

"Well, doctor, Mr. Gregerson never showed up and we don't have enough blood for Mr. Green."

Then Jeff imagined the doctor leaning over and whispering in Mr.

Green's ear, "Mr. Green, I have some bad news — we've run out of blood. The operation is a success and we're sewing you up now, but we're gonna have to send you home a pint short."

There are a lot of people walking around this planet a "pint short." It may not necesarily be a pint of blood — perhaps it's a pint short of love or a pint short of attention. Maybe someone you know is a pint short spiritually or emotionally. Our Heavenly Father calls on each of us to give of ourselves. We may be asked to donate a pint of kindness, a pint of fasting, or a pint of prayer. It usually costs no more than a little time and effort. Look around. There are those walking by who are deficient in things that are just as vital as blood.

Sometimes we get so wrapped up in the things of this world that we overlook our capacities to donate ourselves. There is nothing more important on this earth than people. They are the principals in God's great plan. When we discover that our fellow human beings are "more precious than fine gold" our priorities will undoubtedly become the same as Heavenly Father's.

The Fourth of July, 1976, was a special day, not only because it was the two hundredth birthday of the country, but because I had a wonderful experience as well. The bicentennial committee for Utah had asked if Sun, Shade 'n Rain would donate a free concert as part of the state's celebrations. We talked it over and decided we would. The committee had built a large stage on the grounds surrounding the Salt Lake City and County Building. They put up chairs on the lawn for the spectators they expected. We agreed to perform a full concert, and we knew that it would involve a lot of work. We used our own huge sound system, our own lighting, our own technicians, our own band, our own show outfits — a full concert with all the trimmings.

At this time my dad was back east singing with the Tabernacle Choir as part of the national celebration. This left my mother and my sister Stacy home alone (all my brothers were also gone). Mom and Stacy had decided to go downtown, and while they were on the freeway they heard a radio announcer advertise our concert. My family has always supported my life in Sun, Shade 'n Rain, so mom and Stacy pulled off the freeway at the first exit and came to our show. They were, however, very early and had their choice of seats.

My family sees so many of our concerts that they quickly learn each new song, new joke, and new routine by heart. Generally, they don't even watch the stage as much as they watch other people in the audience. Mom, especially, likes to watch people watch us. It wasn't long after mom's arrival at this concert that she saw a young man walking along the sidewalk. He was in his early twenties and seemed quite interested in our preparations for the concert. He was alone, and he was dressed in a very ragged manner. He wore no socks; his shoes had holes in the bottoms; and the knees were worn out on his pants. His pants were far too short, his shirt was filthy; and his old sportscoat had worn-out elbows. He looked and smelled as if he hadn't bathed in a long time. Mom also suspected that he hadn't had a solid meal in days.

This young man stood with his hands in his pockets, looking at the stage and all the activities. There were chairs being set up and a huge column of speakers were being wired. It didn't take him long to realize that something big was about to happen. He walked up slowly and took a seat. No one asked for a ticket or money, so he knew it was a free show. Since he sat just one row in front of mom and Stacy, he became the target of mom's observation for the whole night.

It wasn't long before most of the seats were filled. The crowds came and found their seats, but not many sat on either side of our young friend. Perhaps it was the smell or just the offensive appearance that kept them away.

The concert began, and mom immediately realized that he had apparently never seen a major production of any kind before. He was totally engrossed in the show. He acted so excited that he could hardly sit still. He laughed, cheered, roared, and clapped his hands through the entire performance.

When he smiled, Mom noticed his teeth or, rather, she noticed what was left of them. Most of his teeth were either broken off or had simply rotted away. The young man was very conscious about his teeth, and sometimes he would slump in his chair and cover his mouth with both hands. He'd look around to see if anyone had noticed, and before long he'd forget his teeth and turn his attention back to the concert. Then after a little while, he'd remember his teeth, stop laughing, cover his mouth, and slump back down in his chair. Up and down he went. Although this routine happened several times, the young man never noticed mom and Stacy.

Mom and Stacy felt sorry for him. They have hearts as big as the sky, and it hurt them to see a young man in such sad shape. They wished they could do something for him. They wanted to help. Mom wondered about giving him some clothes. My family has six boys in it, and we give more clothes to the Deseret Industries than this fellow probably had ever seen. Mom also wanted to buy him some new shoes; she even wanted to give him some money to get his teeth fixed; she wanted to take him and hug him.

Mom told me that the Spirit whispered that she should invite him home for a good meal, a good shower, and some new clothes. It seemed like a good idea, but she couldn't bring herself to ask him. Dad was out of town and none of the boys were at home. It would be too dangerous. Mom and Stacy just sat and kept watching him.

When the concert ended, Sun, Shade 'n Rain was behind the stage signing autographs. This same ragged young man came behind the stage and stood watching us talk to the crowds. We signed autographs on photos, albums, and flyers. Mom and Stacy were just behind the young man, still observing. He didn't say anything, he just stood there for a long time. A couple of times he nearly walked up to ask for a signature, but he never quite mustered up the courage. Tears were in mom's eyes, and she wished that one of us would turn, see him, and walk over to chat with him. None of us did.

As our manager came on the scene and told us it was time to go, I remember saying to the crowd, as I always do, "We have to go now, so I can sign only three more." The crowd pushed forward a little, each person trying to be one of the last three.

When our ragged friend heard me make that announcement, he began to fumble frantically through his pockets. Obviously, he was checking once more for something we could autograph. Nothing was there. He looked around and spotted a garbage can nearby. He ran over, reached in, and tore off a piece of a brown paper sack.

Mom's tears increased as the young man returned only to find the three of us walking away. She told me later that she nearly yelled out loud for me to come back and sign his piece of paper. She must have been yelling pretty loud spiritually, because I heard. I had a strong sensation, an actual feeling, to stop and turn back to sign just one more autograph. So I started back, and as I turned I bumped right into our friend. He was following close behind, and I nearly knocked him over. This was the first time I had seen him. I surprised him so much with my sudden about-face that I could tell he was very nervous. He reached out, handed me the torn piece of paper bag, and mumbled, "It's for my brother."

I don't know if he really had a brother or not; maybe it was just a convenient way to make things easier for him to get the autograph. I remember writing four simple words: "Thanks a lot, Dan." I remember how funny it felt to be signing a lunch sack corner. When I handed it back to him he smiled. I will never forget that smile — not because I noticed that his teeth were in rotten shape — but because I knew I had truly made him happy. He looked as if I had handed him a thousand dollar bill. He thanked me sincerely, turned, and walked away. I felt great inside, and I knew that there was a still, small voice and it had called me back to see this young man.

About this time mom walked up. I was surprised to see her and even more surprised to see the tears in her eyes. "Was our show that bad?" I asked. We laughed, and she began to tell me the whole story about our ragged friend. She confessed that she wanted to invite him home but didn't dare because she and Stacy were alone. I quickly explained that I had no special plans for the evening and would be glad to go home with them. I told her to find the young man and invite him to dinner. Mom looked excited. As she turned to find him, she said, "I knew I should have asked him to the house — I just knew it would work out somehow."

After I had changed clothes, I joined the search. No one could find him. In a matter of minutes he had

disappeared. We even drove through the streets in our cars looking for him, but after an hour we gave up.

That night I wrote the entire episode in my journal. I'll never forget how he smiled and how happy he looked when I autographed his sack. How I wish I could have done more! All I had done was scribble my name on a tiny piece of paper for him, yet he loved it so much. I kept on wondering who he was and where he'd gone. Where did he live? I guess I'll never know. I will just have to be satisfied in knowing that I did a little good. My autograph had been a pint of happiness for him, and I wish I could have given him a gallon.

"Be not forgetful to entertain strangers; for thereby some have entertained angels unawares" (Hebrews 13:2).

I lay in bed that night and couldn't sleep. I opened my Bible and read the story of the Good Samaritan, and it filled me with a warm desire to help lighten the burdens of others. My mind then drifted to the words of one of Joseph Smith's favorite hymns, "A Poor Wayfaring Man of Grief." My experience that Fourth of July permanently affected the way I feel about these verses:

A poor wayfaring man of grief
Had often crossed me on my way,
Who sued so humbly for relief
That I could never answer, Nay.

I had no power to ask his name;
Where to he went or whence he
come;
Yet there was something in his eye
That won my love, I knew not why.

Then in a moment to my view,
The stranger started from disguise;
The tokens in his hands I knew,
The Savior stood before mine eyes.

He spake — and my poor name he
named —
"Of me thou hast not been
ashamed;
These deeds shall thy memorial be;
Fear not, thou didst them unto me."

James D. Miles once said, "You can easily judge the character of a man by how he treats those who can do nothing for him." There are so many people walking around a pint short that we should never let an opportunity pass to help someone. Nothing could be more important. The soul is invaluable, and no activity can have priority over helping souls.

C. S. Lewis reminds us that it is a serious thing to live in a world of possible Gods and Goddesses, that even the dullest and most uninteresting person we talk to may one day be a creature we would be strongly tempted to worship. He suggests that there are no ordinary people; there are no "mere mortals." (*The Weight of Glory* [Grand Rapids, Michigan: William B.

Eerdmans Publishing Co., 1949], p. 15.) We are all a pint short in one way or another, and we are all blessed with unlimited potential.

Just as Sun, Shade 'n Rain are members of a blood assurance program, so each person is a member of Heavenly Father's "love assurance" program. We are called upon regularly to donate ourselves to help save eternal lives. An ancient prophet-king told his people something that is still vitally true today:

Behold, I tell you these things that ye may learn wisdom; that ye may learn that when ye are in the service of your fellow beings ye are only in the service of your God. (Mosiah 2:17.)

Another Book of Mormon passage tells us what God is in the process of doing: "I will make a man more precious than fine gold." (2 Nephi 23:12).

As we look around and see the crowds of lonely and ragged people, let's see them as the fine gold they really are. It's interesting to note that we can give pint after pint of love and not lose any love at all. We can give away and not become any weaker. In fact, the opposite is true. As we serve God by giving ourselves away in service to others, we receive a spiritual transfusion which far surpasses the amount of love we donate to others — to me, that sounds like a pretty good deal.

You Oughta Be

A wonderful stake president (who is also a dear friend) had a favorite saying that he used over and over. In fact, my young friends and I would go to stake conference and make bets on whether or not we'd hear this saying. Sure enough, at every single conference for years, we heard it. I remember looking around the congregation and smiling at my buddies every time the words came from the pulpit. It was a simple phrase that I will never forget. "You oughta be where you oughta be, when you oughta be there." The message is clear, but sometimes the lesson is hard learned.

We oughta take such and such a course in school; we oughta apply for a certain job; we oughta be in sacrament meeting; we oughta attend the temple. On and on it goes. Life is full of "oughta this" and "oughta that." How can we know best which oughta we oughta do? The answer is simple. Ask someone who knows everything. How many people know everything (some think they do), but how many really do? I know of only one source, and that is a spiritual one. Each of us can plug into that eternal source and communicate with powers that do, in fact, know everything. The rest is easy: listen to what they say, and follow the instructions. That procedure will put us in right places at right times for right reasons.

Nearly a year before I got married I attended the wedding reception of a special friend. When the evening came to a close, the new bride flung her bouquet of flowers into an eager crowd of single girls. The girl who jumped highest caught the bouquet and danced around the room believing she'd be the next one married. Then I watched another similar ceremony. Only this time it was the groom's turn. He took the garter off his new wife's leg and prepared to flip it into the air. I learned that any single guy who caught the garter would be next in line to find a wife. It all looked fun, but it was only a fairy-tale game to me. The single men began to congregate, and it looked like it was going to be a football scramble to catch it. I wanted no part of the silly ritual.

I stayed in my chair way over on the opposite side of the room and leaned back ready to enjoy the battle. Casually my mother walked over and tapped me on the shoulder. She commented that I was taller than any of the rest and my chances looked good. "Don't you think you oughta be over there?"

I looked up into her anxious face and replied, "Mom, if the Lord really wants me to get married, he'll help me do it without making me catch a garter. Besides, if it's that serious, he can direct the garter clear over here

and I'll catch it, but I ain't leavin' this chair! No sir!"

You guessed it. The airborne garter went crazy in midflight. It went no where near the huddled bachelors. It landed exactly, squarely, and perfectly in my lap. The loudest scream came from mom, and then the whole crowd cheered and applauded. What can I say? I didn't even reach up for it — it just came. This is a terrible example for illustrating the principle of being where you oughta be. But it's a great lesson on revelation. If a marriage prophecy can come through a garter, then I am convinced that God does, indeed, move in mysterious ways.

That garter turned out to be a prophecy. Not long after I caught it, I moved into an apartment complex, met a girl next door, dated her, and asked her the golden question: Will you marry me? She said yes, and I knew that I had been in the right place at the right time. Her name now is Charlotte Lindstrom. I wonder if she should thank the garter?

One of the functions of the Holy Ghost is to guide and direct toward paths that will put us where we oughta be when we oughta be there. At the same time, the Holy Ghost warns us where not to be. The challenge, then, is to be receptive to his influences and let him lead us where he will. It's exciting to know that the priesthood has the power and authority to bestow upon us a custom-built, twenty-four-hour guidance system known as the gift of the Holy Ghost.

When Sun, Shade 'n Rain was in Hawaii for a concert tour, we heard an interesting story. It dealt with the consequences of ignoring critical warnings. While sitting in a small restaurant having breakfast in Hilo, a city on the big island, we noticed several different lines painted horizontally across the front window. We questioned our little old waiter, who happened to be an active member of the Church, about the lines. He told us that they indicated how high the water level had been during several different tidal waves. One line was about four feet from the ground, another was eight, and the highest was nearly ten feet off the floor. We were amazed and tried to imagine just how much water must have come up onto the island. The waiter continued, telling us that he had lost a daughter years before in a tidal wave. He took time to answer all of our questions about tidal waves, and we learned some enlightening details. He told us that lots of people had died simply because they had ignored the warning sirens.

These are some of the things he taught us about tidal waves. Because they begin far out at sea, they usually don't sneak up. There's plenty of time to warn the populace. As a tidal wave approaches, it can be seen out on the horizon as a long black line. It appears to be standing still, even though it is moving many hundreds of miles an hour. The closer it comes to shore, the more dramatic are the effects on the coastal waters. The undercurrents from any approaching wave pull water back out to sea. The larger the wave, the more water is drawn off the beaches. A tidal wave pulls out so much water that it leaves miles of exposed ocean floor.

For many people this proves to be a great temptation. It allows them to run out onto the barren ocean ground and pick up fish, shells, and all kinds of valuables. Consequently, they ignore the warning sirens because the danger still looks so far away; they think they have plenty of time. The tremendous speed of the wave catches them off guard, and they are instantly gone. They disregard not only the sirens but also the "signs of the times." Not only is the retreating water a sign of danger but the oncoming wave is actually visible, and they prove to be in the wrong place at the wrong time.

It's easy to say, "Well, they deserved it. Their greed killed them. Besides, if they were careless enough to take a chance and ignore the warnings in the first place, then they got just what they had coming." Often, however, we all find ourselves in their same situation — not in facing a tidal wave, but in ignoring the spiritual sirens that tell us we're in wrong places doing wrong things.

Hawaii is a terrific place for lesson-teaching experiences for Sun, Shade 'n Rain. On our second tour to the islands we tried to prove what great surfers we were. All of our concerts were put on at night, so we had our days relatively free. We enjoyed shopping, sightseeing, and, most of all, playing in the ocean. None of us had ever become very good on a surfboard, but we did a lot of body surfing. This is done by using the body as a surfboard. A person simply makes himself stiff and waits for a wave to break, and then he rides into shore on the crest of the water.

It was a lot of fun, but the waves were much bigger than we were used to. In fact, we were body surfing on the largest waves in the world. We were at Sunset Beach where the world championship surfing contests are held. There we were, Utah desert rats, body surfing in deadly waters.

All of the water that comes crashing onto any beach eventually needs to get back out to sea. Generally, the outgoing water forms a powerful current that is called a riptide or ripcurrent. It's just like a river moving against the waves, and the riptide carries anything in its path with it. It is invisible and very dangerous.

Several members of the group swam out a good distance from the shore and floated around waiting to catch a big wave. Two members of our band were out so far that a local surfer floated over to them to see if everything was all right. They told the experienced surfer that they were just fine, and so he left them. Gradually, however, our band members drifted into the riptide and were suddenly carried out toward the horizon. They fought and fought, trying to swim out of its powerful grip. Just when they were ready to give up because of exhaustion, the lifeguard reached them. They all struggled together and made it back to shore.

When everybody finally settled down and the terror of the near disaster had passed, we thought about a powerful lesson we had learned — not only about surfing, but about life. The ocean of life can work with a person by letting him catch a wave and ride it safely home, or it can lock him into a riptide and pull him further and further away until it's everlastingly too late. The eternal lifeguards are always on duty and they save many lives. But people still get so caught up in the currents and trends of the day that they are carried out to a point where even the lifeguard can't reach them.

We can never afford to be in the wrong place on purpose. Life allows us to get mixed up enough as it is. We should never intentionally go where we oughta not be.

One of my favorite Sun, Shade 'n Rain stories concerns a day when we never seemed to be in the right place. We tried and we tried, but we were always "here" when we should have been "there." The story begins in Oregon with us performing for the grand opening of a new hotel. It was a very successful Saturday night concert, but we had to be back in Salt Lake City to speak at a fireside the next day. Our schedule looked perfect since it would take us only two hours to fly home. In fact, we all planned to be back home in time to attend our separate priesthood meetings Sunday morning. We had to get up at 4:30 A.M. because we wanted an early start. We wanted to avoid any problems while checking in our luggage and equipment at the airport.

First, we had a quick stopover in San Francisco. At least it was supposed to be quick. There was a thick fog and so we circled, waiting for a break in the clouds that would let us land. We circled and we circled. Two hours passed, and the pilot finally announced that we were running out of fuel. No problem — he said we'd fly over the bay, land in Oakland, refuel, and fly back to our holding pattern over the San Francisco airport. All went well, and soon we were back circling again and waiting for a chance to land.

Suddenly there was an opening and we landed. Everyone was glad to be back on the ground, even if we were hours behind schedule. All nine of us ran to the airline's counter to find out what our next step was. Our connecting flight to Salt Lake City had taken off hours earlier, but the airline people were helping us reschedule. We were worried about our fireside commitment, and our situation looked even worse when we were told that there were no seats available for Salt Lake City. Our manager, Joe, and the airline host began checking with other airline companies, and luckily they found nine empty seats — aboard a plane that was just ready to leave. It had been delayed by the same bad weather. As luck would have it, however, the boarding area was at the opposite end of the airport. They said they'd wait for us and off we ran — nine upset, sprinting musicians. Our mad dash through the terminal ended as we breathlessly approached the counter and identified ourselves. Our new host said, "Oh, yes, we've been waiting for you. Follow me, please." It was so good to finally be headed home. He took us through a doorway and led us to a waiting bus. A bus? Our airplane was waiting for us across the bay, back in Oakland where we had just been.

We piled into the bus and sat quietly with the fifty other passengers who had the same problem. Everyone was in the wrong place at the right time or the right place at the wrong time. It was nice to see San Francisco from the ground, but that's not where we wanted to be. Suddenly our bus sputtered, coughed, and gave up the ghost. We were on the freeway when the transmission broke down, and we rolled to a stop on an exit ramp.

Everyone looked carefully at everyone else. Undoubtedly we were all remembering the story of Jonah. Remember that on the ship the crew cast Jonah into the sea because his sins were causing all their problems. When Jonah went overboard everything calmed down to normal. Who would we cast out of the bus? No one left but the driver, who hiked to the nearest phone and called for help. Again we waited and waited. At last another bus rolled up and we were off again.

This time we made it. The new bus drove us right out onto the runway, and we climbed directly into the plane. The day was nearly gone by the time we landed in Salt Lake, so we went directly to the fireside wearing the same grubby clothes that we had put on early that morning. For us, the most comical part of the whole day occurred when the airlines apologized to the frazzled passengers of that flight. Our captain's voice came over the intercom saying, "We realize it's been a long day, and we're really sorry about the inconvenience. We apologize and invite all of you to have free champagne, compliments of the airlines."

At least at the pulpit that night I had the satisfaction of knowing I was at the place I was supposed to be. Usually it's not that difficult to get to right places at right times. One definite way to avoid most problems is to stay close to the Lord by developing a listening ear and a quick response to the Holy Ghost's instructions. Those instructions might come via the scriptures, the still small voice, or the voices of our inspired leaders. The following story illustrates how listening to leaders in the Church helps a person avoid the pitfalls that come from being on the wrong paths.

Sun, Shade 'n Rain took part in a youth conference at beautiful Squaw Valley, a year-round resort in California. We performed a Friday night concert, played for the dance afterwards, and then stayed overnight to teach some classes and workshops the next morning. The morning activities ended; and though we hated to leave, we had to get to Reno to perform for a convention.

Reluctant to see us go, the conference people invited us to stay long enough to have lunch — they were serving the meal on top of the mountain. We accepted the invitation, rode the tram up, and there joined nearly four hundred young people and their leaders for lunch. The leaders had scheduled two hours for the lunch break, and then everyone was expected to meet in a large building down by the parking lot for a testimony meeting. After our relaxing meal, we lined up to ride the tram back down the steep slopes. We were nearly the last of the LDS youth, since most of them had already headed for the testimony meeting.

Later as we were driving to Reno we heard a shocking news bulletin on the radio. One of the cables had snapped and sliced right through a tram car at Squaw Valley, killing four people, hurting dozens, and stranding over seventy in midair. They were suspended halfway between the upper and lower tram terminals, a hundred and fifty feet above the ground. Rescue efforts continued all night long. As we monitored the events on our motel televisions we discovered that the tram car that had been ripped open was the car right behind the one we had used to get off the mountain. Had we hesitated a moment longer and decided to catch the next tram, we would have been right in the middle of all the trouble. Right place? Right time? Not only for us, but for all the kids that were in the testimony meeting. A simple schedule by the leaders had placed hundreds of Latter-day Saint young people out of danger.

Several years ago our concerts required some special effects that were prerecorded and controlled from the sound board. One song was a mellow, thought-provoking tune called "Rainbows." We used recorded thunder and rain to help the audience paint mental pictures of a storm. The other song was a comedy number called "Cab Driver," an old Mills Brothers hit. This song ended with the playing of a tape recording of screeching tires, breaking glass, and crumpling metal. I introduced the serious mood for the rainbow song by sitting on a stool with my guitar and telling the folks where, how, and why I had written the song. The setting was perfect, the cue was given, and our sound man plugged in the wrong tape. My gentle strumming was joined by sounds of a car crash. The audience looked unsure, but I kept right on with my tune. Mel and Jeff were laughing under their breath as I tried to keep a straight, controlled face. The sound man immediately recognized his mistake and corrected it on the spot.

I am convinced that life is a wonderful, exciting experience. Life lets us choose where we want to be. Our free agency allows us the right to decide. Our Heavenly Father counsels us and guides us so that we can discover where we oughta be and when we oughta be there. If we follow his suggestions, we will never get a "car-wreck tape" when we need a "rainbow tape." The Spirit will do his part if we do ours. He will draw near unto us only as we draw near unto him. The nearer he is and the more influence we allow him to have in our lives, the less chance we will have of one day saying, "Oh, I shoulda been where I shoulda been, when I shoulda been there!"

Life

Life is a campus of learning,
It's a test, an exam I must pass.
I must struggle and cry
I must fail and retry
It's a climb to the top of the class.

Life is the school I applied for.
And I passed on the entrance exam.
And so, I was born
On a latter-day morn
In an honors class called Abraham.

Life wasn't meant to be easy.
Yet often I hear me complain,
"My homework's too tough,
I've suffered enough!"
Excuses start falling like rain.

But soon I get back to my studies
And laugh at the fool I have been,
Thinking life owed to me
My Godhood — for free —
And I'm rededicated again.

To graduate takes many hours
Of study and action combined;
To learn and to grow
To give and to show
My love for my God and mankind.

So, the next time I feel like complaining,
Instead, I'll pretend I have won.
I'll imagine I see
My Godhood degree,
A diploma entitled: Well Done.

I Could Never Love You More

Every morning
When I arise,
I never see the sunshine
Or the dawning of the skies.

Instead, I see your picture
As I waken to your smile.
So I just lie there
And I daydream for a while.

What a beautiful beginning,
And my heart is very sure
That I could never, ever love you —
No, never love you more.

I work all day,
So very hard I try.
But (then) the problems and the
        pressures
Start to mount as time slips by.

But when I get discouraged
You float into my mind,
I have to stop and smile
At the gentle peace I find.

I look at those around me
And again, I'm very sure
That I could never, ever love you —
No, never love you more.

Then, I get to see you
In the mellow evening light,
Even standing near you
Makes my life seem, oh, so right.

Now day has ended,
We've long gone to bed.
I guess I should be sleeping,
But I'm full of thoughts instead.

My heart keeps singing,
Everything's so good.
I love you more
Than I ever thought I could.

Now the tears are in my eyes
Like many times before,
I can't believe it's growing
I love you even more.

Jacob and Rachel

I grew up with heroes,
The Bible was their home.
Like David and Goliath
Or Sampson and his bone.

And there was good old Daniel
Who walked the lion's path
Or Solomon and his wisdom
Or Moses and his staff.

And now that I am older
And so in love with you,
I found another hero
That felt the way I do.

A man who loved his lady
And Jacob was his name.
Each time I read his story
I always feel the same.

And Jacob loved Rachel.
And he said,
"I will work for seven years."
So he worked for seven years
Because he loved her.

And Jacob loved Rachel
But they said,
"You must work for seven more."
So he worked for seven more
Because he loved her.

My heroes in the Bible,
A lesson they all learned,
That anything worth having
Was something to be earned.

Like Jacob and his lady
I know what I would do;
I'd work for seven years two times
To show my love for you.

So Jacob loved his Rachel
In all the special ways
And said, "The years were nothing —
They seemed like only days."

Now, when I think of heroes
And how I want to be
I think of you as Rachel
And Jacob would be me.

(See Genesis 29:9-30.)

A Single Entertainer's Plea

Where are you?
Please, love, won't you help me find ya?
Where are you?
Don't let the lights and the music blind ya.
Where are you?

I live in a world of music
With the lights and the crowds and the fun.
Curtains rise, show goes on,
Ovations when we're done.
Make 'em cry, make 'em laugh,
Then give my love with an autograph.
They shake my hand and disappear,
I cry, "Don't go!" but they never hear.
No more fans, no microphone.
It's time to leave — I drive home alone.

Where are you?

Another reservation,
Catch a plane and fly away.
Leave behind anyone I find
And promise to return someday.
Another town, a new hotel,
A routine that I know so well.
Concert fever's in the air,
I reach for you, but no one's there.
I look in the mirror 'n see my best friend,
"I guess it's just you and me again."

Where are you?
Please, love, won't you help me find ya?
Where are you?
Don't let the lights and the music blind ya.

Won't Ya Go Out with Me?

There's one thing that I just hate,
The ordinary ways people ask for a date.
Well, I found something and I'm quite sure
You've never been asked this way before.

I'm asking you out as a serenader,
Then you can give me your answer later.
The thing I have planned — it calls for two —
I know that I'm one, I hope the other is you.

Oh won't ya, won't ya, won't ya please go with me?
You see, I can't go alone.
Won't ya, won't ya, won't ya please go with me?
If you don't, I'll just stay at home.

I made me a list, 'bout a hundred names long,
I had to choose the very best.
Well, it took me three seconds and I'd made up my mind —
Won't ya, won't ya please say, yes?

Going out with you would be a lot of fun.
The problem is how to get the asking done.
I'm really not shy, but there's hesitation
And that's why I sent a singing invitation.

It'll be great, just you wait and see.
You know, if I were you I'd sure go out with me.
Now I'm leaving it all up to you
'Cause I've done everything that I can possibly do.

Won't ya, won't ya please say, yes?

My Friend

I talked to a very good friend
of mine about you last night.
The advice he gave seemed so
simple and beautiful and true,
I just had to write it down.

He said, "If she likes you, not
because of this poem; not because
of your looks or lack of looks;
not because of your songs or time
or effort, then she loves you!

"If she wants to be with you, help
you, and do things for you simply
because you are you, then she
loves you!"

He concluded, in the words of
President David O. McKay:
" 'If you meet a girl
in whose presence you feel a
desire to achieve, who inspires
you to do your best,

and to make the most of yourself,
such a young woman is worthy
of your love.' "

I mentioned to my friend how I
would like to have him meet you.
He said, "I already know her."
I smiled, said good-bye, got
up off my knees and went to bed.

(Inspired by something my mother
read to me. I asked her how to
recognize real love, and she read
from the writings of President David O.
McKay, *Gospel Ideals*, p. 459.)

Dan with his wife, Charlotte, and Elder Paul H. Dunn

To a Star

Count the stars
On a quiet crystal nght
And you'll begin to see

A gift of love
Sprinkled across the skies
Into eternity.

There are more stars
Than sand in the ocean,
And each one, I'm sure, has a name.

They were placed there
Like diamonds in darkness,
Worlds of celestial flame.

So I raise my eyes,
Can't see them looking down,
And wish that I could be

A fire in the sky
To point the way back home
For all who want to see.

Some stars
Are brighter than others
With light spilling out from within.

These are the ones
That we wish on
And lean on again and again.

So take my thanks
You unfalling star.
I will try to be

A mighty light —
The way you are —
So other souls can see.

The first star
I'll put in my heaven
The brightest and best it will be.

It will shine out on all of creation.
My first star
I'll name Marie.

(Dedicated to Marie and all
the Osmonds for their tremendous
examples.)

She's Gone

The colors fade,
The rainbow's gone.
The sunset dims,
Night comes on.

The evenings cry,
The night winds blow.
A tear. A sigh.
No place to go.

Drifting through
My troubled mind —
Where to land?
A place to find.

Forever echoes
Show her face.
Here! There!
Can't erase.

A snowflake falls,
It's beauties last,
Though she melts
Into the past.

Now she's gone
I can't pretend.
Final frame
Says: The End

Fireworks left
A cloudy sky.
I am a man,
And men don't cry.

Now she's gone
It starts to snow.
Getting late —
It's time to go.

Buttoned coat,
Scarf, just right.
Wonder what's on
T.V. tonight.

At home with the guitar

Open Your Eyes

Listen to the music,
Watch my thoughts appear.
Open your eyes
So your heart can hear.

Listen to the feelings
Deep inside of me.
Open your eyes
And see me.

If you're tired of being all alone,
Open your eyes and see me.
If you're tired of searching for a home,
Open your eyes and see me.

If you're tired of roaming around
And you wanna make the move
From the lost to the found —
Just open your eyes and see me.

If you're tired of playing the game,
Open your eyes and see me.
If day after day your life is the same,
Open your eyes and see me.

If you're weary and feeling low,
You can come to me.
When there's no where else to go,
Just open your eyes and see me.

There is nothing that I wouldn't do,
'Cause I know what you're going through
The choice is yours — I have set you free
So open your eyes and see me.

If you're tired of hand-me-down feelings,
Open your eyes and see me.
If you're tired of lies and concealings,
Open your eyes and see me.

I'll understand, though you turn from me,
I love enough
To wait patiently,

Until you open your eyes.
Open your eyes and see me.

Against the sky

Rainbows

There never would be a rainbow
If at first there was no storm.
There's got to be clouds of sorrow,
Or the colors will not perform.

If you never have times of trouble
When your dreams get washed away,
Then, you never can earn the rainbow
That you want so bad today.

There'd never be a star to wish on
If, at first, it didn't get dark.
You'll never earn a fiery glory
If you only deserve a spark.

If you wanna feel safe and happy
There's a price that you have to pay,
Or you never can earn the rainbow
That you want so bad today.

Some folks stay discouraged
And it keeps their spirits low.
They ought to be up and fighting
While they still have time to grow.

There always will be a sunrise,
But, first, there comes the night.
Remember the words: We'll prove them
To see if they choose the right.

So if you find there are clouds around you,
Keep on moving anyway.
And you'll find you've been under the rainbow
All along the way.

(Dedicated to Tami Milius)

Dan's solo

Relaxing at a wedding

A New Day

Stillness,
Blackness,
Chillness,
And calm.

Birds sing,
Announcing
The coming
Of dawn.

I watch the light
Spilling over the mountains
So far away.

While Mother Earth
Is giving birth; Congratulations,
It's a baby day.

So many beautiful
Things to see.

A day's one appearance
In all history.

Faces in silhouette

Me 'n My Guitar

One of my best friends is my guitar. We've spent many hours together — just the two of us. We've travelled all over the world together. We've shared the good times and the bad times. We've been close through the successes and through the struggles. My guitar has often soothed my soul, and I have changed its strings. We've held each other and laughed, and we've shared each other's tears. During the happy moods we've made happy music, and during the sad moods we've made music on lonely beaches and in quiet rooms.

My guitar was with me when I first told my wife, Charlotte, that I loved her. My guitar was with me when I sang at a good friend's funeral. My guitar has joined me in welcoming new babies into the world by serenading mothers at hospitals and in singing congratulations to couples beginning their fiftieth year together.

I'll never forget the time I boarded a plane and flew one way while my guitar joined all the luggage and went another way. It was a frightening experience. I couldn't have done our concert that night without my old guitar. Sure, I could have rented or borrowed another one, but it wouldn't have felt the same. The reunion was sweet, and it was just in time for our show. Now when we travel by air, I keep my guitar up front with us people.

My guitar and I begin our story

together with the approach of my fourteenth birthday. I was always active in music, and I remember writing simple little songs when I was just a tiny tot. I would always make my family sit and listen to me sing each new tune. When I reached school age, I loved the singing times. I also recall singing the harmony parts in Primary opening exercises. Finally, I reached junior high school and became part of the school choir.

It was during these junior high school years that I started my career as a performer. One Sunday morning as two of my friends and I were walking home from Priesthood meeting, I invited them over to hear a new record I had just purchased. I'll never forget the song or the artist. It was called "Dreamer," and it was written and sung by Neil Sedaka. My two friends Clive and Steve joined me in listening to my new, catchy forty-five record. We started singing along, and we learned the song by heart. That was the start. My first trio was born that morning. Clive (who later became the musical director for Sun, Shade 'n Rain) told us that he knew where he could borrow an old guitar that wasn't being used. Clive with his magical ear had it tuned in no time, and then he used the hit-and-miss method to experiment with chords. He learned to play the guitar right on the spot.

Before long Clive had figured out the correct chords for "Dreamer," and we added singing in three-part harmony. We ran upstairs and performed our masterpiece for my family and our visiting home teachers. The next thing we knew, we were singing at our ward for the annual elders quorum Christmas party. That was the first of a lifetime of live performances.

It was nearly a year before we returned that borrowed guitar. Clive was able to get several new guitars, and he let me use one of them. He began teaching me some basic chords. I learned fast, because I had to — I didn't like standing in front of audiences without being able to play.

As my birthday approached, I put in a request for a guitar of my own. No more borrowing, no more getting permission from others to play and practice. I wanted my own instrument. My parents and I shopped, and I was horrified to find out what a good new guitar cost. My parents couldn't afford it, and I knew they couldn't.

My birthday came but the guitar didn't. I think I received clothes instead. I tried to be an adult and not show my disappointment. A week passed, and I had completely forgotten about my birthday and had put to rest any hopes for a guitar. It was evening when mom pulled into the driveway with a station wagon full of groceries. As usual she carried a load in with her and sent me out to bring in the rest. I opened the car door, but I didn't see any groceries. Instead, I saw a brand new guitar case. Where there's a new guitar case, the chances are pretty good that there's a new guitar. I opened the case and gazed upon my first guitar. My very own guitar. It was beautiful and very expensive. Looking back at the house, I saw the entire family watching me out of the windows. They were laughing and clapping at my surprise. I don't know how my parents made the purchase, but I was determined to make their investment a good one.

I loved my first guitar. I practiced on it every day. I performed with it. The two of us became good friends during an important period of my life when I was making changes. I was discovering so many new truths about life, and my guitar seemed to be part of all those discoveries. I was learning what was important to me in the world, and certainly my music was. My family and friends became more important during those teenage years. Since school, grades, sports, girls, social acceptance, and music were all becoming new, exciting dimensions for me, I wrote about them and I sang about them.

Another powerful truth began to grow within me during this same period of my life. It had to do with the Church and my testimony. That testimony was born and began to grow. Just as it was with my own guitar, I was finally getting my own testimony and depending less and less on borrowing from others.

Most of my reflective thinking was done when I was alone, but my guitar was always right there. I have often compared my testimony to my guitar, as unusual as that may seem, and have found many similarities.

Item one: A good guitar is expensive. I have, over the years, counseled many of my students to plan on spending a considerable amount of money for their first guitar. The reason is simple: the better instruments cost more. The better the guitar, the easier it is to play, the more beautiful are the sounds it produces, and, consequently, the faster the students will learn. They not only learn to play faster, but they keep the instruments longer and are happier with their own progress. A cheaper guitar invites quick failure, and the instrument usually ends up gathering dust on a closet shelf; and the money which could have been an investment is wasted.

So it is with a testimony: Finding the true church and gaining a testimony of it sometimes involves a lot of shopping. It requires praying, searching, and studying. The philosophies of men come in all shapes and sizes and cater to all kinds of life-styles. Sifting through them to find that "pearl of great price" is an expensive effort. It costs time to pray, and it takes work to keep the commandments. A testimony doesn't just come — it is earned, and, once acquired, it must be kept alive and growing with continual work. Oh, how it is worth it! Once a person has played a spiritual guitar by experiencing a testimony of the living God, it is impossible to settle for anything less.

Item two: Every good guitar needs a good case. It needs protection. Generally, cases are the unexpected expense that new guitar buyers overlook. Cases are, however, an absolute necessity. It would be stupid to pay a lot of money for a beautiful instrument and then to leave it exposed to the elements. Unlike a piano, a guitar usually is carried from place to place and it needs to be guarded. Guitars fall, chip, crack, knick, and even break — and each little "hurt" negatively affects the guitar's performance. No talented guitarist would ever dream of leaving an exposed guitar on a front porch during a snow storm. He wouldn't leave it where thieves might find it. He wouldn't leave it in direct sunlight very long, nor would he ship it on a bus without a case. It would not survive being thrown around with the other baggage. It would have to have a sturdy, protective case.

So it is with a testimony: A testimony needs protection, too. It should always be guarded against those influences that would weaken and destroy it. Why take a testimony to a filthy movie? Why let it dwell on thoughts and actions that would scratch it and mar its strength? Why expose a testimony to life-styles directly opposed to it? It will get bumped enough on its own — it doesn't need any extra hazards. A testimony can influence thousands of people when it's in tip-top shape, but one careless step can break it in two. Repairs often are more expensive than the purchase, and they usually require a long time in the repentance factory.

Item three: Most guitars have six strings, and every one of them is important and needed. A guitarist must use all six strings, or he wastes the potential of the instrument. A guitar, however, can still be played with fewer strings. Occasionally, I have to play with only five strings when one string breaks in the middle of a song during a concert. I can get by, and most of the audience doesn't even notice. But I do. One of my fingers is hitting an empty spot where a string should be. I am sure the audience would notice the weakness of the chord structure and the lack of volume if I broke two strings at the same time. The facts are simple — if all the strings aren't there, then the guitar won't do what its creators designed it to do. The performance will be inferior.

So it is with a testimony: There are many parts of a testimony that might correspond to the strings of a guitar. A testimony is made up of strings, such as tithing, prayer, home teaching, and the Word of Wisdom. A testimony has more than six strings, but each one is vital. The "sacrament attendance" string can't say to the "love your neighbor" string, "I have no need of thee." Alone, a string might seem insignificant; but a testimony cannot perform at its best without every string in its place, doing its job. If my "temple attendance" string was completely gone, my testimony would be less effective. And if all the strings were gone, my testimony would be as dead and useless as a stringless guitar. Even though we can get by with a few missing strings, it seems silly to just get by when we can have full and complete eternal sound.

Item four: When I was a guitar teacher, I felt frustrated when a student had learned a guitar technique that had to be unlearned. Some things are learned wrongly; and even though they work, they need to be undone before the student can progress any further. It was often easier to take on a beginning student instead of one who had learned a little on his own.

So it is with a testimony: There is a lot of sense in the scriptures that admonish us to teach children while they're young. Learning the right way the first time is always easier. A testimony that is built on a wrong foundation or that leans too heavily on others will surely fall. Children who learn to pray, attend meetings, partake of the sacrament, and who enjoy family home evenings are in a much better position to progress to higher laws.

Item five: One of the first topics beginning guitar students must understand is the theory of sound and pitch. A string vibrates, and that vibration produces a certain note. Increase the number of vibrations, and the pitch goes up; lower the number of vibrations, and the pitch goes down. The frets on the guitar help determine how fast a string vibrates: Theory is one thing — doing is another. A student frequently picks up a guitar, places his finger on a given string at a given fret, strums the guitar, and gets only an ugly thump sound. Almost all beginning students get thump or buzz sounds. The goal is to eliminate the thumps and buzzes and to get a beautiful, clear ringing tone. A thump indicates that the student's finger is absorbing all the vibrations because he isn't pushing down hard enough. A buzz means that he is doing better but still has to push harder to keep the string from vibrating on a fret. Finally, when the student pushes hard enough, the clear sound rings through. As students learn chords (playing more than one string at a time) they also learn how to isolate those awful thumps and buzzes and how to correct them.

So it is with a testimony: The different strings of our testimony need to be pushed hard and correctly so that they will sound loud and clear. Each thump indicates a dead string which needs immediate attention. Too many thumps and the testimony dies. Some parts of a testimony only buzz, which means that they are alive but not doing too well. A testimony built on thumps is like a member of the Church who is only going through the actions — movement, but no spirit. A testimony built on buzzes is like the person who is active in the Church, but does only enough to get by. The buzzy chord is recognizable, but not beautiful. Like the guitarist, a testimony holder must find those thumps and buzzes and then try a little harder to get rid of them.

Item six: As a teacher, I could always tell which students practiced and which did not. Practice, not wishful thinking, really does make perfect. The serious students wanted to learn and were a joy to teach, while others only showed up to their lessons because mom made 'em. Being a good musician isn't handed to anyone on a silver platter. The students who stuck it out soon found that the instrument was easier to play, and they began doing things they'd never dreamed of. That ability came only with good hard work, good instruction, a good guitar, and a lot of patience.

So it is with a testimony: Making a testimony grow strong and proficient requires the same four ingredients: good hard work, good instructions, the true Church, and a lot of patience. Faith really can grow into a perfect knowledge. We were put on this earth to prove ourselves — to see if we would practice. It's our choice whether we practice on our testimonies only on Sundays or only a half hour a day. If we practiced all the time, however, we would surprise ourselves at the improvement and we would prepare ourselves for advancement into those upper-division courses that await the faithful. Practice, practice, practice!

Item seven: I will never forget those feelings I had when I got my first guitar. I was so excited that I showed off every little thing I learned. I'd gather my family around and play every new chord I had learned. They seemed like great masterpieces to me. One time I stayed up until two in the morning to finish learning a song. I was so proud of myself that I packed up my guitar, slipped out of the house, ran down to my best friend's house, and woke him up. He had a hard time looking and acting excited about hearing my new chord progressions. Even now, I get all excited to share my new songs with someone.

So it is with a testimony: If a person has cultivated a healthy testimony, he will be just as excited to share that testimony with others as I am to share my music. New converts, especially, have this powerful "sharing" desire. They often feel like running down the street at 2 A.M. and waking up a neighbor to yell, "Hey, guess what? I just heard about a man named Joseph Smith, wait till you hear what happened to him." If I could have converted my "guitar" excitement into "testimony" excitement, I would have been another Paul. Missionary work is one of the spiritual strings I'm still working on. What great guitarist would avoid sharing his hard-earned gift with others?

Item eight: My final comparison is perhaps the most important. Without this last element, every guitarist's efforts would be futile. A person may have the most expensive handmade guitar in the world; he may have the nicest, strongest case to protect it; he may have the very best quality strings; he may have eliminated every single thump and buzz so that his performances are perfect; he may

practice all day, everyday; and he may have a concert schedule that would allow him to influence the crowds of the world — but all these would avail him nothing if he were not in tune.

So it is with a testimony: Any single string out of tune will sour the whole chord. Any facet of life not in tune with the God of testimonies will gradually decay the rest of the "chord of life." Tuning is simple, yet indispensable.

Our Heavenly Father wants us to turn our lives into beautiful instruments that he can use. He is our most valuable and least expensive teacher, and he is always available.

Oliver Wendell Holmes said: "Many people die with their music still in them. Why is this so? Too often it is because they are always getting ready to live. Before they know it, time runs out."

Tagore adds: "I have spent my days stringing and unstringing my instrument, while the song I came to sing remains unsung."

My guitar and I have learned much together, and we plan to experience and learn a lot more. It's an exciting way to live. Let's follow our dreams and focus on the beacon light. President Spencer W. Kimball wrote:

My plea therefore is this: Let us get our instruments tightly strung and our melodies sweetly sung. Let us not die with our music still in us. Let us rather use this precious mortal probation to move confidently and gloriously upward toward the eternal life which God our Father gives to those who keep his commandments. (*The Miracle of Forgiveness* [Salt Lake City: Bookcraft, Inc., 1969], p. 17.)

Let's listen to the advice of our noble teachers. Our spiritual guitars are too valuable to ignore and our testimonies too beautiful to put up on the shelf. Let's get them down, tune them up, and start playing.

Sun Shade 'n' Rain

When You Burp

When I was a little boy, I enjoyed going on business trips with my dad. We spent many hours together in the car, and we talked about everything. During one such road trip when I was only five or six years old, I had something on my mind and I needed to talk about it with my dad. Sitting down together on the edge of the bed in a motel room somewhere in Nevada, dad and I had an important man-to-man visit. Even though it was a simple question, it seemed very important to me. I turned and seriously asked, "Dad, when I burp and I'm in a room all by myself, do I have to say 'Excuse me'?"

Dad didn't laugh, and he didn't tell me what a dumb question I had just asked. Instead, he thought for a moment. Then he taught a great lesson with his answer. "Yes, I think you should say 'Excuse me' every time," he replied, "and I think there are two reasons why you should. First, the room will never be completely empty. You'll never be alone, because your Heavenly Father is always there. He's always watching and he always knows what you're doing. Second, it's good practice. If you can learn to say 'Excuse me' when you're by yourself, then you'll always be sure to say it when others are around."

Needless to say, I have never forgotten that answer. As a little child I understood perfectly what he was saying, and today his message is still coming through loud and clear. If I am a good example to myself, then I will automatically be a good example to those around me.

During my school years I often used dad's "burp counsel" to help me. Whenever I was tempted to cheat on an exam I recalled his words, pictured my Heavenly Father looking over my shoulder, and I overcame the temptation. It worked every time.

The scriptures have verified the truth of what dad said:

The eyes of the Lord are in every place, beholding the evil and the good. (Proverbs 15:3.)

But behold, verily, verily, I say unto you that mine eyes are upon you. I am in your midst and ye cannot see me. (D&C 38:7.)

An experience with Sun, Shade 'n Rain retaught me this lesson. We were performing on the Cabaret stage at Harrah's Club, on the shores of beautiful Lake Tahoe in Nevada. Sometimes we performed for capacity crowds; at other times the room was empty. There was a clock built right into the stage floor. It told us exactly when to start and when to stop our shows. The sets had to be right on schedule whether there was an audience or not.

One night there wasn't a single customer in front of us, yet we went on with the show as if the place were packed. We sang to empty space, laughed at our own jokes, and said thank you to make-believe applause. I remember commenting, "I've never worked so hard for nobody before." Afterwards as we climbed the stairs to return to our dressing rooms, we noticed our boss sitting in his office. We poked our heads in to say hello, and he complimented us on a terrific show. We were shocked and had no idea he had seen the show. It surprised us even more to find out that he had watched our entire show from his office. The stage had a hidden camera that flashed a closed-circuit picture to the television on his desk. He was well aware that the room was empty, and he was watching us to see how we'd react. He was pleased, and we signed a contract for a return engagement.

If a man can sit in an office and monitor our performance on the stage in another part of the building, it's very easy for me to imagine my Heavenly Father's ability to do the same thing. He can and does monitor our lives, and he's interested in seeing our performances on the stage of life — especially those performances played to no audiences.

Another Sun, Shade 'n Rain experience taught me a great deal about example. One week about Thanksgiving time we were performing for the grand opening of a new lodge at a famous ski resort in Colorado. The first night turned out to be a disaster for us. The audience was hard to reach. The people seemed to be ignoring the entertainment completely; and each night got progressively worse. It was one of our first nightclub experiences, and we struggled to get through each show. As our last day approached, we were very anxious to leave. This was one experience we wanted to finish and leave behind.

Finally the last show of the last night was about to begin. We were surprised to see a family walk into the room. There were several young children, and they sat at a table near the front. We became rather excited because the kids, at least, couldn't drink, and they might listen to our show. Then another family came in, kids and all. We couldn't believe it; the father of this family was the owner of the club — our boss. They sat near the front, too. Next came the mayor of the town with, you guessed it, his wife and children.

Our show began as usual, but the audience was different. This time there was no drinking, no smoking, and no talking. Everyone was paying attention. On the spot we decided to plug in some Primary songs for the kids; we did "I Am a Child of God" and "Give, Said the Little Stream." Everyone loved it, and we were feeling better than we had all week.

The show "felt good" and was moving right along when we spotted two policemen. They were standing at the back of the room. I nearly choked. They were looking around as if searching for illegal minors on the premises. The room was full of kids. Instead, it turned out that they were looking for a table, and when they saw one they motioned toward the lobby and in walked their families — children and all.

Afterwards our natural question was, "Why so many families?" When the owner came over to pay us, we asked him. "We have been watching your shows all week," he explained. "We were surprised and pleased to see a clean act, and we knew this was your last night. Even though your show isn't geared for children, we wanted our families to see you before you got away."

Later that night as the group discussed the show, we each felt bad. We had moaned and groaned all week long. We had complained that no one was listening and that no one cared whether we were on the stage or not. Yet, all the while, the most important and influential men in the community were not only watching but taking notes and judging us. We were lucky that our attitudes hadn't drastically affected our performances.

Life often is the same way. We ask

ourselves, *Is it all worth it? Is anybody watching? Does anyone really care about my performance?* I know and testify that it is worth it, that we are being watched and judged. When there's no applause, we must continue to perform. We need to stand tall, announce to ourselves, *I Am a Child of God,* and think of that great day when we will get all the applause and rewards we have earned.

Many times Mel has told fireside audiences that each of us is an example whether we want to be or not. That example may be good or it may be bad, but it will be radiated to those around us. We are always showcasing our lives in front of others. Our best bet, then, is to impress ourselves. As with dad's burp advice, if we can perform well when we're alone, then in public exposures we will stand tall. If we're proud of the one in the mirror, no matter who is or who isn't watching us, our Heavenly Father will be proud of us. An Osmond poem illustrates:

Mirror, mirror on the wall
I don't like your life at all!
How did we ever get to be
The kind of person that I see?

Mister, mister Look-alike,
Don't we both want what is right?
I wanna change, but can't you see
You're the one who's stopping me!

Do you think no one will see?
Don't forget, you can't fool me!

(From the Osmond album, *The Plan.* Used with permission.)

I am convinced that good habits, good life-styles, and good communication with the powers of eternity begin within each of us. If we truly are content and happy with ourselves, then we can share ourselves with others. Only then will our examples project an influence of good on others. The words from the hymn "Let Each Man Learn to Know Himself" express these same feelings.

Example sheds a genial ray
Of light which men are apt to borrow,
So first improve yourself today
And then improve your friends tomorrow. (*Hymns,* no. 91.)

"Be a good example" is easy to say, it's easy to type, and it's easy to think about. But sometimes it's not so easy to be. Many fireside crowds have heard me say those very words from the pulpit: "Be a good example." Even after giving such noble instructions, I sometimes go out into the "real" world and live as though I'd never heard the words. Permit one such example.

I spent an afternoon with some friends, and we decided to go to a movie — an R-rated film. We had an entire list of reasons why this particular movie would be okay to see. This was in Salt Lake (where I was becoming well known), and the longer we stood in line, the more nervous I got. I began hoping that no one would see me. When we reached the ticket window, the girl behind the glass handed me my ticket, leaned up to the little hole, smiled, and said, "I really enjoyed your fireside the other morning. You spoke at our early morning seminary devotional, and it was great. Enjoy the movie."

I felt terrible, but I smiled back, thanked her, and hoped she didn't know which show I was going to see. (There were four theaters, and she knew exactly which ticket she'd sold me.) I was committed, so we proceeded to the ticket taker. The young man tore each of our tickets in half, and when he got to me he told me how much he had enjoyed our fireside. Then he directed us to the correct theater. As we hurried down the corridor, I heard him yell over to the popcorn girl, "Hey, that's one of the guys in Sun, Shade 'n Rain!"

By now I was a four-foot midget in a six-foot-four body. Just as I started to relax, the flashlight girl showed us to our seats and whispered to me that she had liked my talk. I didn't enjoy the movie and to this day I don't remember what it was about, but I do remember the example I was setting. It's haunted me ever since.

My talks on example and my actions on example just didn't go together, and when they compete the actions are much louder than the talks.

A Sun, Shade 'n Rain tour took us into southern California. One of our Los Angeles concerts was with a gentleman named Regis Philbin. He was a powerful entertainment critic for the huge local newspaper, he was the host on a popular talk show, and he was a great entertainer. Since we were going to appear with him in concert, he invited us to be on his talk show. This was exciting for us because we'd be interviewed in front of millions of people. It wasn't every day that a group was able to appear on the show "A.M. Los Angeles," and so our manager wanted us to be thoroughly prepared. Joe drilled us with all kinds of facts: where we were performing, how many albums we'd cut, and where the albums were available, etc. We memorized the answers and reported to the studio. We had been in front of many television cameras, and so we weren't nervous.

Finally everything was ready — our makeup was just right, Joe was anxiously standing in the wings, we were sitting on the couches next to Regis, and the interview commenced. The little red light came on, and we were broadcast into millions of living rooms. I felt proud, confident, and relaxed until Regis asked his first question. "I understand you fellows met and started Sun, Shade 'n Rain while you were on missions for the Mormon Church. What do you do on missions?"

I was closest, and I was caught completely off guard. Joe hadn't prepared us for missionary discussions. I don't know if the camera was on me or not, but I did know that I was turning red — millions were waiting to hear my answer, but my head was swimming with a million unrelated thoughts. *What do I say? How should I say it? What was the question? Man, my throat is dry. Millions of people? I'm getting redder. Is that Joe passed out on the floor? Hey, Jeff, why don't you butt in and answer? If I don't look at Regis, he'll go away.*

All the time I remained cool, calm, and collected on the outside. Inside, however, I was a wreck. Jeff did answer immediately, although it seemed like eternity to me. "Well Regis," Jeff began, "on missions we travel to an assigned place somewhere in the world, and we spend two years at our own expense teaching people. We teach them about the Mormon Church, we clear up some of the misconceptions people have about the Church, and, mostly, we just teach people what we believe."

I smiled, sat up a little taller and was super proud that *we* had answered so smoothly. Regis had his second question ready, and it ruined me more than the first one had. "And what do you believe?" he asked. As I started falling apart again, Mel jumped in with, "Regis, we believe in God and in Jesus Christ. We also believe that there is a living prophet on the earth today, just like there was anciently. It's pretty exciting to teach people about it."

Again, I was thoroughly proud. Our interview gradually curved toward the entertainment world as we discussed standards and survival in the music industry. It was then that I finally came alive with some comments of my own, but I will never forget how nervous I was when Regis caught me off guard with those questions about the Church.

I never want to be caught off guard again. I want my example to be ready twenty-four hours a day. I don't ever want to have to plan to be a good example. The Savior was very definite when he said:

Ye are the light of the world. A city that is set on an hill cannot be hid. Neither do men light a candle, and put it under a bushel, but on a candlestick; and it giveth light unto all that are in the house. Let your light so shine before men, that they may see your good works, and glorify your Father which is in Heaven. (Matthew 5:14-16.)

And then again in 1834 the Savior reminded us of that same responsibility "to be a light unto the world, and to be the saviors of men" (D&C 103:9).

I am grateful for the many examples I have had in my life. I am mindful, also, of where my talents come from and why they were given to me. My desire is to magnify them and multiply the gifts entrusted to me so that I can return them tenfold. I am also thankful for the scriptures and the prophets who teach us more and more about him whose perfect example should be held far out in front of all the rest. I am thankful for a wonderful family and especially a father who took the time to teach his son that example is important in private as well as in public.

I am most thankful to the Savior for living the way he taught. His words and his actions left a powerful message. His example teaches us to be examples, and his life tells us to say excuse me even if no one else is in the room.

Meeting President Ford

Little Things

Sun, Shade 'n Rain performed a concert in the high school auditorium of a small town in Idaho. It was a standing-room-only evening, and we were happy with our performance. During the concert the three of us poked fun at each other, which worked well as part of our comedy routine. At one point Mel and I teased Jeff about his solo, and he acted upset and even pretended he was crying. He said things such as, "Nobody loves me; you guys always pick on me, and you always ruin my solos." The audience roared with laughter, and Jeff acted out the part more intently.

Everyone enjoyed the concert except one little girl. She was sitting on the third row near the front, and she never laughed. In fact, it looked as if she was crying. When the show was over, we went to our dressing room and almost immediately heard a knock on the door. Our manager ushered in a young mother and her daughter for us to meet. We recognized the daughter as the little three-year-old girl from the third row. Joe introduced Tiffany and her mother. Tiffany was still sad, and the tears kept sneaking out. Then the mother explained what was wrong. "Tiffany was upset through your show, and I think you should know why. She thought that you guys really were picking on Jeff. She thought Jeff really was crying. She thought that the audience really was laughing at Jeff. She really thought nobody loved Jeff, and she has something that she wants to say to him."

Then the little girl slowly walked over to Jeff. Jeff got down on one knee to meet her, and she threw her arms around him, gave him a big hug and kiss, and told him that she loved him. There was a special spirit in the dressing room that night as we all choked back the tears.

What a wonderful lesson we learned from Tiffany! She saw someone who needed loved and attention. From her point of view no one in the audience was going to help Jeff, and so she did what had to be done. She didn't care what anybody else thought. She didn't worry about her mother or the rest of us in the group — she just wanted to make Jeff feel better. Her actions showed us what pure love was. She reminded us of the verse that says we all need to cultivate such pure love.

Verily I say unto you, Whosoever shall not receive the kingdom of God as a little child, he shall not enter therein. (Mark 10:15.)

To qualify for entrance into the celestial kingdom we need to learn how to become as a little child and be able to express love and appreciation to others. Tiffany expected nothing in return for her deed of kindness.

It may seem a little thing to tell somebody that they're loved — a few moments and a few words. But it's those little things that count eternally. Tiffany didn't perform a miracle and she won't make the headlines, but her act of sensitivity will live on in our hearts. I am convinced that any one of us could easily have done what Tiffany did — back when we, too, were three years old. But now that we're grown up, it's a little tougher. We've learned how to suppress those Christlike instincts, and this suppression has calloused many of our feelings.

The Spirit might whisper, "That person is having a bad day — go over, put your arm around him, and tell him you love him. Tell him you appreciate his friendship. You'd better hurry or you'll miss the chance; go, do it now!" Then we talk back to those promptings and think *Oh, I can't do that! What will he think? I've never done it before — I can't start now. I'd be too embarrassed; besides, he already knows I appreciate him. He's in a bad mood anyway and doesn't want to be bothered. I'll do it some other time.* Before we know it, the opportunity is gone and the Spirit has whispered in vain. How many times will the Spirit try to talk us into something if we consistently talk ourselves out of it?

Often it's difficult to see the little

things in their proper perspective. We usually don't have time for the little things because we're working too hard on getting to the celestial kingdom. Alma tells us that this isn't right; "Ye may suppose that this is foolishness in me; but behold I say unto you, that by small and simple things are great things brought to pass" (Alma 37:6). Then, as if to make sure we got the message, the Lord tells us again in the Doctrine and Covenents to "be not weary in well-doing, for ye are laying the foundation of a great work, and out of small things proceedeth that which is great" (D&C 64:33).

We all know the big things, and we could list all the major commandments. But what about a pat on the back or a helping hand to a brother in need? These are the often-overlooked little things that slip right by us. Getting to the celestial world won't happen in one giant "mother-may-I" step but, rather, in little steps. Progression is reached "here a little and there a little."

Little drops of water,
Little grains of sand,
Make the mighty ocean
And the beauteous land.

Little deeds of kindness,
Little words of love,
Make the earth as happy
As the heav'n above.
("Little Things," *Sing with Me,* B-49.)

There is a small club in Nevada where we regularly perform. We enjoy it there even though the stage is small. It gives us a chance to be down close to the audience. During one two-week engagement we were contracted to do two shows per night. There was quite a long wait in between the two sets, and I spent that time watching people. That's right, I'd run to the dressing room, change clothes, and go to my favorite spot to watch the casino crowds. I found a little out-of-the-way corner where I had a good view. It fascinated me to see all the different ways people reacted to winning and losing. Each night I spent an hour or so studying those who stood around the gaming tables. They were always wrapped up in their own worlds, and watching them proved to be quite entertaining.

Along with studying the patrons, I watched a lot of the employees, most of whom we had already met. After a few days of crowd-gazing, I spotted an employee that I didn't know. She was a nice looking woman who worked the roulette wheel. She was amazingly good at handling people. They enjoyed her personality and were attracted by her pleasant manner. There was always a waiting line at her table. One day she looked up and caught me staring at her. I smiled, and she returned a beautiful smile.

Before long one of the other employees came over to talk to me. He was a friend of ours, and he had noticed the exchange of smiles. He told me that she was married to the pit boss and that she had a reputation of being very cold and unfriendly with fellow employees. He went on and on about how hard she was to get to know, how nobody liked her, and how I ought to steer clear and save myself some problems. Several other employees told me the same thing, which really surprised me. She seemed to get along with everybody when I was watching. Her smile seemed nice enough. But I decided that everyone else must have known something I didn't, and I thanked them for their information. I never would have guessed that she was so unfriendly.

Several days later I was walking through the casino to get back to the stage for our second show. I'll always remember that it was Monday because the place seemed so empty. The staff told us that every week began slow, and it was normal to have a dead Monday (but I figured the crowds were all home for family home evening). All employees, including the roulette lady, had to stay at their stations even if nobody was gambling at their table. It was house policy. I had to walk right by her to get to the stage.

I wanted to say hello, but my mind flooded with things I had been told: "Don't talk to her; she's unfriendly; stay away." I was holding two Almond Joy candy bars I had just got from a vending machine. (By the way, it's the only gambling I did — I'm convinced that the candy bar vending machine is programmed just like the slots, sometimes it takes the money and says, "Too bad! Try again.") As I approached the roulette wheel I really wondered if I should say anything to her. I wanted to, and finally the entertainer in me pulled through and I stopped and looked right at her. I was at a loss for words until I remembered my candy bars. I held them up and said, "Can I bet these on black?" "Sure," she laughed, "put 'em down." I put them on the black area and watched the little ball spin 'round and 'round. It surprised us both when it fell into a black slot, and I was a winner. She looked kind of embarrassed. "What do ya know," she exclaimed, "you're a winner and I don't know how to pay you." We were joking all along; and I picked up the candy bars, told her not to worry about it, and walked away. I remember thinking that she sure was friendly for being so unfriendly. I wondered why everybody else was so down on her. She was either a great actress or my friends were all wrong.

The story continued several days later when I saw her in the parking lot. She was taking a break and sitting all alone on the bumper of a car. It was late at night, and I was walking back to my motel room. I wanted to say hi, but again I heard those voices saying, "Don't talk to her, she's unfriendly." I got worried that maybe she really was a grouch — it was her break, and she didn't have to be nice. I talked myself out of acknowledging her, and I walked right by. She didn't even look up. I felt so ashamed that I made myself turn around, walk back, and say something, anything. Before my courage failed I said, "Excuse me, but I just wanted to say hello and tell you that I think you've got a great talent. I've watched you a lot, and you are excellent at handling people. I also think you are a very pretty lady." She smiled and thanked me. "You're welcome, goodnight," I replied, and then I turned and walked away feeling 100 percent better. It was so easy. And, despite my fears, she didn't bite my head off.

Then the story moved to our last night. It was just before our last show, and I had some of my Salt Lake friends visiting. They came over to see us on closing night. I always enjoy having my pals with me on the road. I had taken them to my favorite watch-the-crowd spot, and we had a good time watching the Saturday night mobs. They, too, noticed my roulette lady and asked if I knew her; and even though I really

didn't, I boasted that I did. I wanted to impress my friends — until they asked to meet her and get a picture with her. Then I got worried. I didn't even know her name and had only talked to her two brief times. Lucky for me, it was too late to meet her — it was time to start our last show.

When it was all over we went to the coffee shop for a bite to eat. Our sound equipment was being torn down and loaded into the trailers. We had an all-night drive ahead of us. As we visited around dinner, one of my buddies tapped me on the shoulder and whispered, "Guess who just walked into the coffee shop?" I had no idea; but as I turned around and saw the roulette lady standing in the doorway looking around the room, I felt uneasy. My friend continued, "She's probably looking for you, Dan." I laughed at the silly thought and hoped she didn't accidentally walk by. I didn't want to make any introductions.

There came another tap on my shoulder as my friend said, "I think she sees you, she's headed this way." She did, in fact, come up to our table. She came so fast that I couldn't collect my thoughts, and before I knew it she was gone. Without a word she handed me a large brown sack — a sack full of Almond Joy candy bars, my winnings from the roulette wheel. The club hadn't purchased them, the roulette lady had. There was also a card and a beautifully wrapped gift in the sack.

First of all, I ripped open the card and looked at the bottom to find out if she signed it. I wanted to find out her name, and for the first time I called her Bette. My friends definitely were impressed. I said things like, "Oh, yea, Bette and I are good friends." I enjoyed my buddies saying "Ooh" and "Aah." The card thanked me for being such a gentleman musician, and the gift was a wooden plaque inscribed with a poem about the importance of smiles and friendship.

I was the first driver that night, and I thought about Bette for a lot of miles. I had been so wrong in my judgment of her and wrong in listening to what others said about her. I knew I should have been a better missionary. I could have been a better friend. Two simple things, a smile and a compliment, had impressed her enough that she took time and went out of her way to give me a card and gifts.

If I could have lived the two weeks over again, perhaps I could have talked to her about the Church and changed a life; instead, I was too worried about what others said. Like Tiffany at the beginning of this chapter, I shouldn't have cared what others said.

It truly is the little things that count —

"Let no man count them as small things" (D&C 123:15). It's the "I love you" and the "thanks for being my friend" that really mean the most. Bette's plaque is hanging on my wall and her card is in my journal. They are there to remind me that smiles and compliments work wonders. The small deeds not only build our own self-image, but they build the images of those around us.

I Never Even Said Hello

I was the last of the group members to get married, and I will never forget how the gang tried and tried to get me "hitched." They were always introducing me to every girl within hundreds of miles. Even when we were on tour they didn't let up. One time in Las Vegas we went to see Wayne Newton's show. It was our night off, and we wanted to see and study this great entertainer. There was a long waiting line for his show, and while standing there I enjoyed watching the people down in the large casino area. I felt good that night because it was my birthday and the gang was treating me to dinner and the show.

Remember, I was still single and I was doing my own searching and looking at girls. Suddenly I spotted a beautiful girl clear across the room. I wished that we were closer so I could get a better look. She began moving in our direction. As she got closer, I saw that she really was a pretty girl. The others of Sun, Shade 'n Rain were all wrapped up in their conversations as I gazed secretly at the approaching girl.

Gradually I began to get nervous. Not only was she moving in our general direction, but it appeared that she was aiming directly at us and, more specifically, right at me. I should have been excited, but instead I was nervous. I wondered if I knew her from somewhere. I even tested her by looking away and then peeking back to see if she was still coming toward me — she was. I knew that I didn't recognize her, and I also knew that I was about to meet her.

As she walked up to me I didn't know whether to smile, shake hands, move out of the way and let her pass, or what. Everyone around me had backed off, leaving me the obvious center of attention. They were laughing at my dilemma. They all knew something that I didn't. She came up to me, looked into my face, and asked, "Are you Dan?"

My throat was dry, but my voice cracked a feeble yes. Then she asked if it was my birthday, and when I nodded she threw her arms around me as if we were long lost friends. She gave me a big kiss right on the lips. I know I turned bright red as the surrounding crowd cheered and applauded my lucky circumstance. I never thought to ask her name. I just smiled and waved as she said good-bye and left.

The group had found this girl, a total stranger, and paid her five dollars to pull this stunt on me. I've always been happy to know that she walked right over to Jeff and gave him back his five bucks. It was a great birthday surprise, and for years after that I spent my birthdays with Sun, Shade 'n Rain standing in large crowds,

smiling and looking around. It never happened again.

I use this story as an introduction to another girl and a special experience which happened during my first year at the University of Utah. As a freshman I took lots of general education courses — one of them was music appreciation. On that first day I just sat and looked into the faces of the three hundred students seated in the semicircular room, trying to see one I recognized. Instead I saw the face of a girl that I wanted to get to know. I paid special attention as the roll was being called, and I jotted down her name when she raised her hand. I had never had a problem meeting people or finding things to talk about, so I hurried over to her side as soon as class ended. I got right up to her and froze. I chickened out. I went blank. I didn't know what to say or how to act. Luckily she hadn't noticed me, and I took an easy way out. I rationalized that I'd see her five days a week for the whole quarter. I'd meet her tomorrow or the next day. I could wait.

I ended up waiting a long time. I was just as chicken the next day and the day after. I don't know why, but it was hard for me to break the ice with her. I couldn't bring myself to say hello.

I was at home one night when I spent some time thinking about how

I could get her attention. I started laughing right out loud. She was only a girl. What could possibly happen. It couldn't hurt any worse than I was already hurting. My self-confidence was a wreck. I made up my mind to quit procrastinating. I would meet her the next day. My mind was made up. (It's always a good feeling to make a commitment.) I would meet her no matter what.

I was up early, picked out my best clothes, put on my best cologne, and got ready in record time. I didn't want to be late. This was to be a special day. I felt confidence surging through my body as I walked into the classroom. I took my seat and watched and waited. She never came. I couldn't believe it. I felt so high that I knew I could talk to her just the same tomorrow. My hopes were up all day long.

Later that evening I was home watching the news on T.V. Suddenly, I saw a picture of *her* face flash on the screen. I had stared at her long enough — I recognized the face immediately. The report went on to tell of an automobile accident and the life it had claimed. She had been killed on the freeway that very morning. She died going to school, to music class.

I sat for a long time in silence. The day I was going to say hello was the very day she left this life. I went into my room, closed the door, and

thought and thought. I wrote my feelings into my journal, entitling the entry "I never even said hello."

I learned that a person can't wait for anything. Life is too precious, and it is so short. I made a commitment in my journal that I would never again avoid talking to someone or miss a chance to say hello. I would never pass up an opportunity if I could help it to do something nice for someone. Why? Because we never know which "someones" won't be around tomorrow.

It's a sobering thought to realize that any one of our friends might be called home at any time. Any one of our loved ones may suddenly leave this life. Most sobering of all is the thought that any one of us might pass to the spirit world when we least expect to.

I will never forget the first time that I seriously thought about death. I was a little boy, and our family was returning from a visit to grandma and grandpa's house. Although it was close to midnight, the sky was bright red in color, everything beneath it looked pink; it reminded us of a beautiful sunset, but it was in the eastern not the western sky. We were amazed, and I was somewhat frightened as we drove along. Mom and dad, not exactly sure what was happening, began talking about some of the signs of the last days and the end of the world. That did it! My little-kid mind went wild, and I stretched out on the back seat in terror thinking, *Oh, no! It's the end of the world, and I'm only a little kid!*

I tried to fall asleep. I knew that the world could go ahead and end just as well if I wasn't awake to be part of it. If the world was over, I wanted to die in my sleep. There was one problem — I couldn't fall asleep. My heart, I remember, was beating too hard.

Finally the radio announcer broke through the static and talked about the beautiful northern lights that filled the Utah skies. It sure felt good to sit up, look around, and know that it wasn't the end.

I had never really thought about death and dying before. I had never thought about the end of the world nor any other eternal topics I heard my folks discuss that night. For the next several weeks I didn't sleep very well. My little mind was tossing and turning with thoughts of "forever" and "death." One night my fears made me sit straight up in bed. I was too young to fully understand gospel principles, and yet I was old enough to be frightened by thoughts of eternity. All I could picture while trying to grasp eternity was darkness and endless nothing. I began trembling and perspiring.

I had a birthday coming up, and I was young enough that I had looked forward to the party for weeks. That night even the excitement of a birthday party was overshadowed by my new fears. I remember wondering to myself, *What if I should die?* My fears grew: *There'd be no more birthdays. No birthday next year or the year after that or the one after that or after and after and after.* I couldn't relax, and I began to cry as my mind went on, *No more mom, no dad, no friends, no visits to grandma and grandpa forever and ever and ever.*

It was one of the worst nights of my life — a traumatic experience I will never forget. It was the first time that my childhood faith had been attacked by my questioning mind. I wanted answers. I wanted to understand. Finally I settled down enough to remember my parents and what they had always taught me. I climbed out of bed, still in the middle of a trembling nightmare, and got down on my knees. My prayer was short and simple: I wanted to relax and go to sleep and not be afraid anymore. My Heavenly Father heard and answered. The evil cloud went away, and I went right to sleep. A little boy learned that God lives; he hears and answers prayers. My fear of death left me that night, and it has never returned.

As I grew, so did that tiny testimony. I learned how to understand things about eternal life and immortality. My fear of "nothingness" turned into love. I learned more about God, and I learned that I'd never be alone again.

I'm sure that the girl in my music class didn't plan to have an accident on the freeway that morning. She didn't leave home saying, "Bye, mom, I won't be home for dinner tonight." We can only hope and pray that she was prepared to leave this life. We can hope and pray that each of us will be ready.

Something that Og Mandino wrote in his book *The Greatest Salesman in the World* helps me to keep in the proper frame of mind about death. One of his ten scrolls in the book says:

I will live this day as if it is my last. And if it is my last, it will be my greatest monument. This day I will make the best day of my life. This day I will drink every minute to its full. I will savor its taste and give thanks. I will maketh every hour count and each minute I will trade only for something of value. (Og Mandino [New York: Frederick Fell Publishers, Inc., 1968], p. 78.)

May we all be so busy and so anxiously engaged in good causes that we can pause in eternity, look back at our brief visits on earth, and say as did Jacob, "the time passed away with us, and also our lives passed away like as it were unto us a dream" (Jacob 7:26).

May those dreams be beautiful memories, not nightmares. The Lord tells us that this life is only a fleeting moment and that we are in the midst of a test. Death is not the end of life and the beginning of nothingness. It's only a doorway out of the classroom. And when we've finished the class, we can look at the answer sheet. The grading will be final, and there will be no make-up exams. May we all get straight 'A's and graduate with honors.

There are people we need to say hello to. There are lives we need to touch. There are improvements we need to make and goals we need to set. There are things we need to repent of and habits we need to break. And today, not tomorrow, is the time.

At the Homecoming Parade, BYU Hawaii

Lights, Camera, Action!

Most people are glad to take off for a couple of weeks when they get a vacation. I'm glad when we come home. Concert dates can keep Sun, Shade 'n Rain on the road for months at a time. That's probably why I felt so relaxed being back in Salt Lake, standing in line with a girl I liked (back in my single days), waiting to see a popular space science fiction movie.

The line was long, and we had time to talk and time to think. My mind wandered to parts of section 88 in the Doctrine and Covenants. The content didn't strike me as funny, but I laughed at myself for pondering scriptures while on a date.

Verses 108 through 110 talk about a great revealing that will take place on the judgment day during which all the acts of our lives will be shown "to all living." They even mention that our "thoughts" will be revealed as well as the "intents of our hearts." Somehow, our life's journey will be recreated to prove that the judgment is just. When I was little, I heard teachers try to describe this revealing as an epic motion picture on a giant screen.

I'd never really thought about that before and, now, all of a sudden it really struck home. Thoughts came rushing into my mind: like, What if there really was a recording being made of my life? What if there really was a movie being prepared that showed all my actions, all my thoughts, and the intents of my heart?

I imagined that it would probably be entitled *Dan Lindstrom on Earth.* A quick survey of my life led to some powerful realizations: Would I be half as excited to stand in line to see my movie as I was to see this movie? Would I want to take my family and friends to see it? Would I invite the bishop and the Savior?

What started out as a simple thought evolved into deep reflections about my life and the motion picture I would make. The concept remained in my mind long after the real film had ended and I had driven my date home. In fact, I kept thinking about it for weeks. I couldn't shake the concern I felt, wondering what type of picture it would be.

For the sake of illustration let's assume that we each are, in fact, making movies of our lives, and that they will be shown on a huge celestial screen. Be assured that some type of evidence will be available on our judgment day in court; and during this chapter, let's pretend that it's a movie.

President John Taylor said:

Man sleeps for a time in the grave, and by-and-by he rises again from the dead and goes to judgment; and then the secret thoughts of all men are revealed before Him with whom *we have to do; we cannot hide them; it would be in vain then for a man to say then, "I did not do so-and-so;" the command would be, Unravel and read the record which he has made of himself, and let it testify in relation to these things. (Journal of Discourses,* 11:78-79.)

One of the books I read for school had a couple of pages that talked, in a roundabout way, about my movie theory:

The evidence seems to indicate that everything which has been in our conscious awareness is recorded in detail and stored in the brain and is capable of being "played back" in the present.... Perhaps the most significant discovery was that not only past events are recorded in detail but also the feelings that were associated with those events.... *The evoked recollection can be more accurately described as a* reliving *than a recalling.* Another conclusion we may make from these findings is that the brain functions as a high-fidelity recorder, putting on tape, as it were, every experience from the time of birth. (Thomas A. Harris, M.D., *I'm OK — You're OK* [New York: Avon Books, 1973], pp. 25-30.)

My favorite Book of Mormon prophet Alma seemed to agree. He described the judgment day and the great revealing as follows:

for behold, the day cometh that all shall rise from the dead and stand before God, and be judged according to their works. . . . The spirit and the body shall be reunited again in its perfect form; both limb and joint shall be restored to its proper frame, even as we are now at this time; and we shall be brought to stand before God, knowing even as we know now, and have a bright recollection of all our guilt. (Alma 11:41, 43.)

Using the movie analogy, I began to make some comparisons. What is involved in making a real motion picture, and can I apply it to the making of my eternal movie? Every time I watch a movie I pay particular attention to the credits. I watch all the names roll over the screen: the producer, the director, the stars, the co-stars, the writers, and the editors. What do they actually do?

The name in biggest print usually is the star. I suddenly realized that I was the star in my movie. To me, that's fascinating — I will have "top billing." The more I think about my leading role, the more it helps me when I feel depressed or discouraged. Every time I feel like a nobody, I just remember that I am a star; I am important, and somebody, somewhere, is filming me this very minute. The change is instant; I cheer right up and get busy doing something constructive and positive.

I can't afford any poor scenes. I need to be a star all the time, not just in public.

Sometimes, in the oddest places, I suddenly remember that I'm a star. I might be walking down a crowded city street; suddenly I'll laugh at myself, stand a little taller, stick out my chest, and look around wondering, "All right, where's the camera? Is it filming my good side?"

I think a lot about "opening night." I want everyone to be impressed and proud of my life, not ashamed and embarrassed. I like the words that the Osmonds wrote for one of their songs:

You laugh and you smile,
You try to run away.
Don't you know, what you do
You might regret someday?
'Cause there's one who has eyes
On your evil way:
The Movie Man!

You're in living color,
It's your picture show.
Even what you're thinking,
Everyone will know.
That's the day
You'll take the stand:
With The Movie Man!

(From the Osmond album *The Plan.* Used with permission.)

Since everybody is being filmed, everybody is a star. Nobody is a nobody. Judgment day will be that great occasion when our secret good deeds and our quiet efforts will be broadcast and "thy Father which seeth in secret himself shall reward thee openly" (Matthew 6:4).

As I wondered who would be the co-stars in my production, I soon realized that I was in charge of that area myself. I decide who will be in which scenes and how prominent a role each will play. I decide who I associate with — who I date, who I marry, who my friends are. I decide, too, if there will be a lot of scenes shot in local bars or if they will be shot in sacrament meetings. Most movie companies, I'm sure, are very selective when they choose people for parts. They need actors and actresses who will attract praise and help create a superior product. I need to be just as choosy with my supporting cast.

It's not hard to recognize that a producer is very important. His name always appears by itself on the screen. I did some research to find out what his responsibilities are, and I was shocked. The producer generally takes all the risks. He hires the entire staff, and he fires when necessary. He controls the financing and, therefore, takes the greatest gamble. If his film makes it big, he could earn millions; if it flops, he could lose his shirt. Since I am taking all the risks in my movie, I am its producer. I oversee the production

— I am in charge. My movie will either be a story with a happy ending about exaltation, or it will be a tearjerker about a lesser kingdom. One way, I win; the other, I lose. If the final product meets celestial standards and gets good reviews, my investment will be returned many times over. If it fails, who can I blame? I can blame only me, I'm the producer.

There is an advantage, however, in being the producer. I can get all kinds of help. Remember, I do the hiring. The first and most important position to fill is that of director. A director is a person chosen and hired by the producer to direct the cast, especially the stars. He helps them portray the right actions in the right way. He tries to help them feel the part and to act it realistically from within.

There are two directors that want the job. In fact, they want to direct our film so much that they work overtime trying to get our attention. One is Satan and the other is the Holy Ghost. They both have lots of experience, and they both have success stories. Both of them are spirits and, therefore, have a tremendous capacity to direct. They have very different ideas about the direction a movie should go, but the one thing they have in common is price — both are expensive. Satan is willing to jump in and work for free now, but his plan will have us paying eternally. The Holy Ghost, on the other hand, requires his payment right up front. He demands strict obedience to principles of cleanliness and righteous living. In return, he promises top-notch twenty-four-hour service and guarantees a hit the night our movie is shown.

A director is vital to any movie; and as the producer, I need to be very careful in choosing mine. I must decide on one or the other because they will not work together, and then I must pay whatever price is necessary to get and keep my director through the entire project.

There will be no stunt men filling in for me during my show. When the going gets rough and dangerous, I can't holler for a double to take my place. We were placed on the set to experience life firsthand. I can't turn the scene over to someone else — I must act out every frame.

What about an editor? Is there an editor in my movie? I'm sure that there is, if I request it. In a highly technical motion picture many scenes are shot over and over from various angles, and then the best clips are used in the final version. If something doesn't work right the first time, it can be improved upon and tried again. Editors labor strenuously deciding what to keep and what to throw away. As I look back over my movie, I certainly am thankful that

the Lord has given us similar methods for taking out bad scenes and for closing the gaps. The editing method is called repentance, and it's just as effective as the editing done by the man with the razor blade and tape who slices and splices in Hollywood. Anything that's eliminated with the Lord's method is gone forever and is not shown in the final version. It's great to read about the Lord's way of editing our films:

Behold, he who has repented of his sins, the same is forgiven, and I, the Lord, remember them no more. (D&C 58:42.)

. . . though your sins be as scarlet, they shall be as white as snow; though they be red like crimson, they shall be as wool. (Isaiah 1:18.)

But if the wicked will turn from all his sins that he hath committed, and keep all my statutes, and do that which is lawful and right . . . all his transgressions that he hath committed, they shall not be mentioned. (Ezekiel 18:21-22.)

What happens, though, if after editing (repenting) there's not much left of my film? The comedian Bill Cosby once said, "My life flashed before me and the movie was so short, I had to ask for a rerun." If it seems that I might have a movie that's too short or too dull, then I need to become a good writer. Yes, that's right — I am the script man, too. It's my responsibility to make the scenes worthwhile and exciting, to develop the plot and lead it to a glorious climax.

Too many people just sit back and wait for somebody else to make things happen in their lives. They consider life boring; just a simple day-to-day routine. They say things such as "Today turned out to be just like yesterday, and yesterday was a lot like the day before, and tomorrow will be the same." If their life patterns ever change, it will take a miracle; and they don't want to make any miracles happen by their own efforts. It reminds me of Satan in the premortal existence. Even back then he wanted to be involved in our movies. He offered to pre-write all of our scripts. He had it all planned that each of us would come to earth and act out the part he'd written for us. He wanted our lives to fit into his screenplay. We heard his idea, we fought it, and we rejected it. Why? Because we wanted to come to earth and act our own scenes. We wanted to come and prove that our lives could be successful, and we wanted the free agency to prove we could do it on our own.

Regular entries in my journal provide an excellent opportunity for me to write bits and pieces of my script. In it I can record progress on the film. My journal also is the perfect place to list daily goals and to pre-write my scenes before the day begins.

Morning prayers provide an excellent chance to talk with Heavenly Father and to counsel with my director. Together we can plan how to act out the day; and then again in evening prayers I can look over the day and analyze the scenes. Each day should be a powerful and moving episode.

As I contemplate my responsibilities with this movie, I am amazed at the awesome job I have. I am the star. I am constantly in front of the camera. I am the producer and carry a constant awareness that I will make it or break it with this film. I am responsible for hiring other people and for making the payments to my director. I decide on the supporting cast. I need to survive all the dangerous scenes without a stuntman. I serve as my own editor, deciding what to keep and what to throw away. I am responsible to see that effective editing-repentance takes place. I am the writer and, as such, am in charge of making the story line an active and a powerful one. It's a full-time job.

In the film *Man's Search for Happiness* we are told that each of us will be held accountable for every minute of our lives on this planet. Perhaps this means that my movie will not only show what I did, but what I could have done had I used my opportunities to the fullest.

Thinking about that helps me decide to use my time more wisely. I want to become my own critic and to take serious looks at my movie. I want to regularly preview scenes and to regularly review the overall effectiveness of my acting, producing, and directing.

I am very sure that each of us will stand in line and see our imaginary movie (or something like it). I want to be proud of my production. I want to stand tall and be excited to view it in the presence of my friends, my family, and my Savior. I want to approach that "world premier" with my head held high and full of confidence that I will wax strong in the presence of God.

I don't want to be standing in line, scared to death about the inevitable screening. I don't want to be like those that Amulek saw

being brought before the bar of God, to be judged according to our works. Then if our hearts have been hardened . . . then will our state be awful, for then we shall be condemned. For our words will condemn us, yea, all our works will condemn us . . . and our thoughts will also condemn us; and in this awful state we shall not dare to look up to our God; and we would fain be glad if we could command the rocks and the mounains to fall upon us to hide us from his presence . . . But this cannot be. (Alma 12:12-15.)

Alma the younger went through a similar ordeal, and he describes what a terrible thing it was to stand before Jesus Christ and look over some of the bad scenes Alma had in his movie. He wrote:

The very thought of coming into the presence of my God did rack my soul with inexpressible horror. Oh, thought I, that I could be banished and become extinct both soul and body, that I might not be brought to stand in the presence of my God, to be judged of my deeds. (Alma 36: 14-15.)

Alma was blessed, however, and given the chance to repent, to edit those bad scenes. From then on he made his life into one of the most powerful movies this planet has ever known.

We, all of us, still have that same blessing — we, too, can edit and write. Over and over the prophets have declared that this earth life is the time to do our editing and our writing. They tell us that waiting until the end is dangerous; and when we die, then comes that darkness "wherein there can be no labor performed." To me, that means no more filming.

I look forward to seeing your movies, and I want to be proud to show you mine. It helps me to remember the words of Jacob, "Therefore, cheer up your hearts, and remember that ye are free to act for yourselves."

What a tremendous blessing it is to be able to "act for ourselves." Let's get our acts together so that when our day comes and we sit in the great theater in the sky, our movies will get standing ovations and our Father will say, "Well done."

On top of the world